JOB: A Vision of God

JOB: A Vision of God

WARD B. EWING

A Crossroad Book —————————————
THE SEABURY PRESS • NEW YORK

The Seabury Press
815 Second Avenue
New York, N.Y.

Printed in the United States of America

Library of Congress Cataloging in Publication Data

Ewing, Ward B   1942–
Job, a vision of God.

"A Crossroad book."
Bibliography: p.
1. Job, the patriarch. 2. Bible. O. T. Job—
Criticism, interpretation, etc. I. Title.
BS580.J5E87   223′.1′924 [B]   75–45387   ISBN 0–8164–0285–X

TO MILES, JENNIFER, AND LUCIE

CONTENTS

PREFACE

A Noble Book; all men's Book! It is our first, oldest statement of the never-ending Problem,—man's destiny, and God's ways with him here in this earth. . . . Sublime sorrow, sublime reconciliation; oldest choral melody as of the heart of mankind; —so soft, and great; as the summer midnight, as the world with its seas and stars! There is nothing written, I think, in the Bible or out of it, of equal literary merit.[1]

Carlyle is only one of many who have fervently praised the literary qualities of Job. From Goethe to Kant, from Jung to Blake—men of varying interests, vocations, and talents have discovered in this small book one of the supreme achievements of mankind. A book of deep thought and sensitive poetry, portraying the depth of human suffering and the height of God's glory, Job combines the anguish of pain with a passion for truth and a sensitivity to the Being of the Almighty. Job stands alone as a work of literature, human drama, and theology.

Like so many literary classics, Job is known and even discussed, but rarely read. The purpose of this volume is very simple—to help the reader read Job.

This is not a commentary. Very little space is devoted to passage-by-passage discussion of the text. This book is an essay on the meaning of Job, designed to help the reader understand the dynamics of faith and interpersonal relationships that are contained in the poem and to see the relevance of Job's sorrow and his vision for modern living.

The nature of mankind, the enigmatic character of the

world, and the mystery of God do not allow the sensitive author to make simple, clear, and concise conclusions in a portrayal of man's condition. The author of Job was both a man of sensitivity and of deep thought. His conclusions are not simple, clear, or concise. One need only compare any two works on Job to see how scholars of equal competence have produced understandings of the book that are radically different.

It is a bold undertaking to interpret an author whose insight was as profound as that of the writer of the Book of Job. If he has been too deep for others, it is not unlikely that he has been too deep for me.

Perhaps the presumption of age has led me, like Elihu, to add the ramblings of a young man to the already vast library interpreting and analyzing this masterpiece of literature. Perhaps. But I would like to think there is another reason. I am a parish priest. Daily I see people who are sick. I see the elderly growing infirm and facing death. I feel the pain as a husband and wife open their hearts to me describing the difficulties in their marriage. I weep with a struggling young couple whose child is stillborn. And what do I have to offer them? A vision of God. I give myself, and a hope based on the vision of God, a vision that has grown out of suffering, the suffering of our Lord Jesus Christ and the suffering of my brother, Job. I write this book with one primary hope: that those who have not already done so might find a brother in Job, and finding a brother may see with him their God.

We usually think of Job in terms of human suffering. Job is the archetype for all who know loss and despair. But the author of Job also presents in the climactic conclusion of the book a glorious, exultant, wondrous portrayal of God. The author's meaning is not simple. Yet if that meaning is to be discerned, we should not look for it in one part of the book. It is to be found in the full portrait—the pain of man and the grandeur of God.

I recommend reading the Book of Job in one of three versions: The New English Bible, The Revised Standard Version, or Today's English Version from which the book of Job has been published separately under the title, *Tried and True: Job for Modern Man*. The King James Version has many mistranslations, some at crucial places. Other modern translations suffer as a result of a peculiarity of the English language—we have the same form in the second person for both singular and plural. Job speaks to his friends in the second person plural and to God in the second person singular. In Hebrew (or most other languages for that matter) the difference is obvious, but in English there is no difference. The NEB and RSV preserve the distinction by using thee, thou, and thine as forms of address to God. *Job for Modern Man* clarifies whom Job is addressing by adding the word "God" at appropriate places.

I suggest two ways of reading Job: one way is to follow the reading selections I have suggested with each chapter of this book. The other method is, after completing this book, to read Job straight through as one would read a short story.

For those who have cassette tape players, a ninety-minute cassette of Job is available from the Bible Reading Fellowship, P. O. Box 299, Winter Park, Florida 32789. This tape is a reading of the New English Bible translation of Job that I revised and edited.

I was introduced to Job in 1966–67 when I was privileged to spend the academic year at General Theological Seminary in New York City reading and studying the book under the tutelage of Dr. Robert C. Dentan. One of the greatest biblical scholars in the Anglican Church, Dr.

Dentan is a meticulous and thorough scholar who has never lost sight of the fact that the Bible is the word of God. Since that time I have been a parish priest, struggling to continue my studies of scripture in general and Job in particular while being with God's people in their joys, their sorrows, and their worship.

I have found it almost impossible to give proper credit through notes to the scholars of the book of Job. Over the past eight years many of their thoughts have simply become my thoughts; many of their ideas have stimulated my thinking. In place of notes, in the bibliography I have designated those works which I found particularly helpful.

In reading "prefaces" I always skip over the author's acknowledgments of thanks. I shall never do so again. Those persons I here acknowledge are the unseen and unsung workers who have made this book possible. I give grateful thanks to St. John's Cathedral, Jacksonville, Florida; to its Dean, the Very Reverend John F. Mangrum; and to my fellow clergy, the Reverend Matthews Weller and the Reverend Canon George D. Kontos; all of whom carried the burden of extra work to allow me leave to write. I thank Mrs. Albert Brantley for her expeditious typing of the manuscript, and Mrs. John A. Ewing for proofreading both the draft and the manuscript. And I express my deepest gratitude to Dr. Edwin E. Harvey, former Warden of St. John the Baptist Theological College and Canon at Holy Trinity Cathedral, Suva, Fiji, who read the manuscript and offered many helpful suggestions. Perhaps it goes without saying, but the patience and support of my wife, Jenny, who gave birth to our third child as I struggled to birth this volume, has far surpassed even the devotion of the "capable wife" described in Proverbs 31:10ff. I, her husband, sing her praises (Prov. 31:28).

CHAPTER 1

SETTING THE STAGE

The war is over. The anxious parents receive a letter from their son. Relieved and joyful they await his return. But in a battle that need not have been fought, an inept officer made a mindless decision, and an entire company needlessly lost their lives. David's joyful homecoming is not to be. A car of happy, reveling teenagers traveling seventy—seventy-five—hit a bridge abutment. Reporters are the first to find the parents. "There's been an accident. . . . Four kids in a car. Your son. Your daughter. They're all dead." Flash! and the reporters have a picture for tomorrow's front page. A little red toy umbrella, the remaining memento from a beloved doll, pretty red shoes, and a mangled body—all that remains of what was once a happy, young Rebecca, molested and murdered by an idiot. An explosion at the plant costs J. B. his fortune and the life of his only surviving daughter.

Archibald MacLeish in his play *J. B.* portrays the tragedy and the pathos of Job in the unforgettable pictures just recounted. Job's story is not a sweet, sanctimonious tale with a neat moral. His life is a nightmare of inescapable destruction, agony, and desolation. It is far too easy for students of the Bible—lay and clerical—to speak dispassionately of Job's suffering. How indifferently we read the biblical story of Sabeans and Chaldeans destroying Job's livestock, of lightning killing sheep and shepherds, and of a whirlwind striking "the four corners of the house" causing it to fall on Job's children. But beneath the ancient, agrarian storyteller's tale, Job's pain and desolation are real. The Book of Job is no disinterested philosophical discussion. In his agony Job cries out for God to leave him in peace and then for God to vindicate and restore him; he cries out for consolation from his friends and then decries their comforting; he would approach God like a prince and then humbly bows down, the penitent. The Book of Job is the most emotional book in the Bible. How can anyone survive such tragedy? Why should anyone even try to survive?

Any discussion of the Book of Job must be at times unemotional. The investigation of textual problems, the relationship between different parts of the book, the background from which Job was written—these and other problems are all cerebral. They are important, for how one solves these intellectual problems will determine how he interprets the book. Yet beneath any rational and learned exposition of the technical problems of the Book of Job lies the nightmare that is Job's life. We must never disregard the emotional devastation that is found behind every word that comes from Job's mouth.

The dramatic form

The first step in any study of Job is grasping the basic outline and structure of the book. A prose story begins and ends the book, framing a poetic dialogue that culminates in Job's final speech and God's response. The usual and natural division of the book is into five sections:

1. a prologue in prose (chaps. 1 and 2) introducing Job and his sudden misfortunes and introducing the three friends who come to comfort Job;
2. a poetic dialogue (chaps. 3–31) between Job and his comforters;
3. a poetic interjection by Elihu (chaps. 32–37), a fourth friend who surprisingly enters the scene at this point;
4. the speeches of the Lord (38:1–42:6) in poetry addressed to Job and concluded by Job's repentance;
5. an epilogue in prose (42:7–17) recording Job's restitution.

Ever since the rise of modern criticism, certain incongruities and inconsistencies have led biblical scholars to attribute only portions of the book to the original author. A plurality of authorship would imply a plurality of purpose and meaning. If the reader assumes multiple authorship, he usually uses only those portions of the book he attributes to the original author to interpret the meaning of the book. The secondary portions are interpreted as additions countering certain conclusions drawn by the original author. For example, if the speeches of the Lord are considered secondary, then the meaning of the book is sought primarily in the prose prologue-epilogue and the poetic dialogue. How one views the text, then, is essential to how one will interpret the book.

I believe that all portions except the Elihu speeches (chaps. 32–37) and chapter 28 come from the original author and were intended by him to be a part of the book. The following brief explanation of this position is not intended to exhaust the subject nor hopefully the reader. A full discussion about the unity and integrity of the text may be found in most commentaries. A fuller exposition of my views is found in Appendix A.

Clearly chapters 24–28 are deficient. Bildad's third speech (chap. 25) is only six verses long, and Zophar's is entirely missing. Job surprisingly expresses views heretofore espoused by his friends and vehemently denied by him. Some critics regard this as merely an accident in the transmission of the text; others regard it as an intentional changing of the text in order to bring Job to the acceptance of the orthodox view. The text is unacceptable as it stands. All emendations are based on the material in the preceding sections of the dialogue: that which is considered heterodox is assigned to Job; and the orthodox, to the friends. My own thoughts concerning this garbled section and my edited version of the New English Bible translation is in Appendix B. I recommend that the reader either skip chapters 25–28 or that he use the translation in Appendix B beginning with chapter 24.

Chapter 28 is a self-contained lyrical poem on the inaccessibility of wisdom to man. An unlikely speech for Job or his friends at this point, the poem is not related to the previous dialogue nor to Job's speech that follows. While its theme reflects a concern of the author it is not an integral part of the book. Though the poem is beautifully written and worthy of meditation, to preserve the flow of the story, it is best omitted as one reads through Job.

The speeches of Elihu (chaps. 32–37) are rejected as secondary additions by a large majority of scholars. Their style is diffuse and even pompous. The language has important differences from the rest of the poetic dialogue. For example, Elihu prefers the name El to the other divine names, Eloah and Shaddai; while in the rest of the book they occur with almost equal frequency. Elihu is the only

Hebrew name in the book. He is not mentioned in the prologue or epilogue. He appears without warning and disappears without a trace. His speech disrupts the connection between Job's challenge to God (31:35–37) and the divine response (chaps. 38 ff). Elihu quotes from the dialogue and he addresses Job by name, which the three original counselors never did. As one reads through Job, Elihu is best omitted to preserve the drama and continuity of the original.

All commentators on Job recognize the emotional character of the book: the depth of Job's suffering, the anguish of his cries, and the insensitivity of his friends. But few commentators take this emotional character very seriously in their interpretation, and no commentator develops this side of the book to its fullest. A basic concern of this essay on the meaning of Job is to analyze more fully the emotive quality of the book: the emotional interaction between Job and his friends, the development and change of their feelings and personalities as the conflict grows, the internal conflicts within Job himself, and the incredible impact of Job's confrontation with God.

The motivating interaction of Job and his friends has not been developed fully in the past at least in part because of the commonly held view that Job is a philosophical dialogue concerning the reconciliation of the justice of God and the undeserved suffering of Job. Those who so view the book tend to see the following parts being played: The friends represent the contemporary orthodox understanding that suffering is God's punishment for sin. Job criticizes that view by denying that his suffering is caused by moral wickedness. God finally enters the debate, explaining Job's suffering in a way that affirms Job's innocence and also reconciles his suffering with the goodness of God. The meaning of the book, according to this view, is found partially in the speeches of Job and more fully in the Lord's address. The major difficulties of this view are several. Scholars have been unable to agree on the content of the Lord's answer and therefore on the meaning of the book. The dialogue fails to fit the pattern of philosophical debate. And there is no character motivation for Job's and the friends' speeches.

The failure to consider the interaction between Job and his friends on any level other than the intellectual results in a viewpoint summarized by Dr. Marvin Pope:

The dialogue thus makes little contribution to the solution of the problem. Actually it is scarcely appropriate to call this section of the book a dialogue. There is not here the give-and-take of philosophical disputation aimed at the advancement of understanding and truth. Rather each side has a partisan point of view which is reiterated *ad nauseam* in long speeches.[1]

To search for an intellectual discussion in Job is to make nonsense out of the dialogue—over three-fourths of the book. But after all, why should we expect a man who has just lost his children, his wealth, and his health to enter into a philosophical disputation!

I believe the book of Job is more accurately understood if viewed as a drama. When I use the word drama, I do not mean that Job was written as a play intended to be performed. Rather Job is what is technically known as a closet drama—a drama intended primarily for reading and not for viewing. Job is above all a story. A story that has a beginning and an end, a story in which there is movement and character development, a story that develops a conflict, reaches a climax, and then concludes. It is a drama because the action and development of the story is known through what the actors say, not by means of a narrator talking about them. It is a drama because the basic motivating force in the story is the character of the actors as revealed in their speeches. Only a dramatic interpretation of the book is able to fully incorporate the deep emotions present throughout the story.

A diagram of the different parts of the book illustrates the basic dramatic structure.

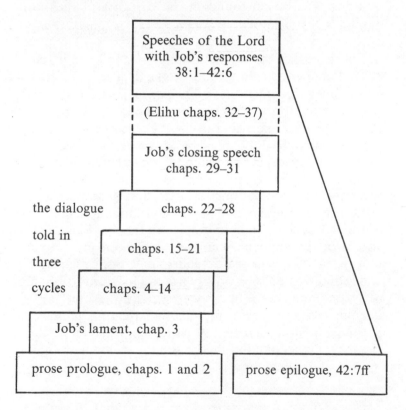

The prologue sets the stage. The drama begins with Job's lament. Then comes the development of the conflict

through the dialogue, culminating in Job's final speech. The
climax is that final speech and the Lord's appearance to
Job. The denouement finds Job repentant and the friends
under indictment. The epilogue concludes the whole.

In viewing Job as a dramatic story, as we shall see, the
meaning is not found in the dialogue, though there are
some beautiful passages there, passages that have great
meaning. Nor is it found in Job's final speech. The
meaning is not even found in the speeches of the Lord.
Basically the meaning is found in the dramatic action
of the story: What is the conflict? Why does it happen?
And what is the result? The meaning of the book is found
in what happens to bring Job to make his final speech, and
what God's judgment is in response. In the dynamic
interaction of Job and his friends and of Job and his God,
we find the dynamic vision of life the author is portraying.
Two basic questions must be answered in the denouement. At the very end Job says, "I repent." Of what does
he repent? He has rightly affirmed his innocence, and he
never accused God of injustice. After Job's repentance, the
Lord turns to Eliphaz and says, "you have not spoken as
you ought about me, as my servant Job has done." The
picture in the dialogue seems to have been that Eliphaz
and the friends were the defenders of God, declaring his
justice and righteousness. Why would God turn to Eliphaz
and say "you have not spoken rightly of me"? The
meaning of the book and the answer to these two
questions is not found in any particular verse or passage.
The meaning is found in the personal development of Job
and the dramatic action of the total book.

Wisdom and the wise men

How can Job survive his tragedy? Why would he even
try to survive the nightmare that has taken from him all he

lived for? The story of Job is the story of how he does in fact survive. It is about his pain, his comforters, and his relationship with God. It is a story for all people in all times. But the author wrote during a particular time and out of a particular philosophical perspective. The Book of Job is one of the biblical books of "wisdom." The author of Job wrote his classic in the context of the answers and consolation his culture and religious perspective would give to the devastated Job. To understand Job—his faith, his hope, his anger and his despair—we must understand wisdom. Then, understanding Job as he was in his own time, we can respond to Job as he is in our time.

The Old Testament wisdom writings are Proverbs, Job, Ecclesiastes (the Hebrew title is Koheleth, translated in English, "the Preacher"), and certain Psalms (including 1, 37, 49, 91, 112, 127, 128). In the Apocrypha we have two wisdom books: The Wisdom of Solomon and Ecclesiasticus (The Wisdom of Jesus, son of Sirach). These writings have been the most neglected in the Bible, at least in our age. The influence of wisdom is not, however, restricted to these books, as the forms and substance of wisdom thought are found in many other places in the Old Testament.

The root meaning of the term wisdom (Hebrew, *hokmah*) is skill or ability. For example in the account of Israel's exodus from Egypt, we read that the men who built the tabernacle were "wise" in the use of wood (Exod. 36:1). This means simply that they did a good job; they were skilled carpenters; they were artisans. Furthermore, the term does not necessarily imply any ethical value. Jonadab is called a wise man (*'iš hakam*, usually translated "shrewd" or "cunning") because he was able to devise a plan whereby Amnon could violate his sister Tamar (2 Sam. 13:3).

We will use the term "wisdom" to refer to the Old Testament corpus of wisdom writings and to the thought embodied in those writings. The root meaning of skill and ability is still important, however, for wisdom is concerned above all else to teach skill in the art of living. The guiding purpose of the biblical proverbs is to enable the student so to order his life that the desired goal of comfort and success is obtained, the feared end of poverty and lawlessness is avoided, and the peace and prosperity of the community preserved.

Although the terms "philosophy" and "ethics" are sometimes used to define wisdom, wisdom should not be confused with philosophy. Philosophy comes to us from the Greek world and strives to comprehend all things through some coherent and consistent system. Wisdom is much more pragmatic and particular. The endeavor of wisdom is not a systematic approach to understanding existence; it attempts to communicate the ability to live successfully.

Medium and message are closely related. Wisdom is written in poetry, philosophy in prose, and that reflects the essential difference. Philosophy seeks to define and analyze through the use of greater and greater precision in its terms. Wisdom undertakes to communicate to the heart and spirit. The basic technique or stylistic method of Hebrew poetry is parallelism—the structure of a poetic verse that expresses one thought in two different ways. In the psalms and all Hebrew poetry the thought is stated in the first half of the verse and then repeated and/or expanded in the second half. Sometimes both halves say the same thing; sometimes the second half will be a negative expression of the theme. The whole poetic principle is to communicate by association, not by definition. By expressing one thought in two ways, parallelism exemplifies this principle of communication by association. The reader of philosophy responds, "yes, now I understand." The reader of poetic wisdom says, "Oh! Now I see!"

The writers and teachers of wisdom are known as "wise men." The wise men are not a group identifiable with one particular function, like priests. Rather, they were the ancient intelligentsia. They were advisors to the king. They taught in the schools and held public offices requiring education. The wise men were an international group of people. They enter Israel's life with the establishing of the monarchy. Every court in the ancient East had its scribes and advisors to the king.

Apparently the wise men in different courts exchanged ideas and writings freely, for wisdom in all the ancient cultures had a non-nationalistic flavor. The biblical wisdom writings, the least markedly Hebraic writings in the Old Testament, express this tolerant, world-wide perspective in several places. For example, the "thirty sayings" in Proverbs (22:17–24:22) are borrowed from an Egyptian work. Today we find great differences between Egyptian and Hebrew religion. But the wise men were able to ignore the differences and bring together the common human elements. In Job in the speeches of the Lord at the end of the book, are descriptions of the hippopotamus, the crocodile, and the ostrich. These are not animals native to Israel, but reflect the international interests of the wise men.

Though it expresses the international flavor and perspective of all wisdom, Hebrew wisdom as a whole does differ from the writings of the wise of other ancient cultures. When wisdom and the wise men were brought into Israel as a part of the structure of the king's court, they entered the Hebrew culture; they came into contact with the strongly ethical religion of the God of Abraham,

Isaac, and Jacob. The story of wisdom in Israel is a story of the growth and adaptation of this tolerant, cosmopolitan system of thought to the intolerant God of Israel, to his prophets and his law. Job is the finest expression of the confrontation between wisdom and Yahweh, the one, true God.

In most of the Bible, the beginning point is God's call, God's covenant, or God's message to his people. With wisdom, the beginning point is observation of the world. The wise men were astute observers of life:

'A bad bargain' says the buyer to the seller,
but off he goes to brag about it.
[Prov. 20:14]

Three things there are which are too wonderful for me,
four which I do not understand:
the way of a vulture in the sky,
the way of a serpent on the rock,
the way of a ship out at sea,
and the way of a man with a girl.
[Prov. 30:18 ff]

The wisdom teacher desired to teach others how to live a successful life. To do this he studied life and began to determine patterns of how some people are successful and some are not. He then developed an aphorism that expressed what he had learned. For example, from the experience of life one learns that if he gets involved in another person's fights he will often get in trouble himself. Out of this experience comes the proverb:

Like a man who seizes a passing cur by the ears
is he who meddles in another's quarrel.
[Prov. 26:17]

Or to take another example, the wise man saw that if a person co-signs a note for someone else, he is likely to be asked to pay it. This observation resulted in this proverb:

> Never be one to give guarantees,
> or to pledge yourself as surety for another;
> for if you cannot pay, beware:
> your bed will be taken from under you.
> [Prov. 22:26 ff]

Wisdom is based, not on revelation, but on experience —on discovering the order in nature, particularly the relationship between action and consequence, and then making choices and decisions on the basis of that order.[2] The Book of Proverbs is largely the collection of such observations that have been expressed in literary form. By reading and learning this wisdom of the ages, the student becomes more skilled in making the right decisions for his life.

Most of the biblical proverbs are concerned with right and wrong action. In some passages, however, the wise men transcend the role of teacher and advisor and articulate the presuppositions behind their teaching. In poems, written centuries after the founding of the monarchy, wisdom is personified as a woman. The most important of these are Job 28 and Proverbs 8.

> 'The Lord created me [Wisdom] the beginning of his works,
> before all else that he made, long ago.
> Alone, I was fashioned in times long past,
> at the beginning, long before earth itself.
> When there was yet no ocean I was born,
> no springs brimming with water.
> Before the mountains were settled in their place,

long before the hills I was born,
When as yet he had made neither land nor lake
nor the first clod of earth.
When he set the heavens in their place I was there,
when he girdled the ocean with the horizon,
When he fixed the canopy of clouds overhead
and set the springs of ocean firm in their place,
When he prescribed its limits for the sea
and knit together earth's foundations.
Then I was at his side each day,
his darling and delight,
playing in his presence continually,
playing on the earth, when he had finished it,
while my delight was in mankind.'

[Prov. 8:22–31]

There is order in the world because God used wisdom in
its creation. In the beginning it was chaos, void, and
without form, and God created structure. He declared that
structure good (Gen. 1). We can observe the structure
wisdom has imposed upon the world. If we will follow
wisdom and abide by the discerned order, then we will
know what to do with our lives and how to make
decisions. The world-view of the wise men is explicit in
their writings: The natural world is regulated by wisdom,
and man must learn to regulate his life by her.

Before the founding of the monarchy, God spoke
audibly to Samuel (1 Sam. 3), was consulted by lot for
every important decision, and had to be appeased constantly by burnt offerings (1 Sam. 13 and 14).[3] This
personalistic, but capricious view of God is absent from
the teachings of the wise. The wise men do not see God
working through the sacred oracle, but discern his will and

character primarily through observation of the orderly workings of creation. This wisdom perspective is not unlike our contemporary secular perspective: man must solve his problems himself through observation and reason. The God who called to Samuel by name is no longer heard in the land. In his place the wise men posit an almost deistic God, who created the world, who established order through wisdom, and who endows man with wisdom to study this order and to make his own choices in directing his own life.

Such freedom and responsibility is fine until one is confronted with irrational and unavoidable tragedy. What help is secular problem solving to Job? How can Job in his pain relate to the God who is known only secondarily through the orderly workings of the world? Job is caught between life and the wisdom-secularist-problem-solving perspective. More than any other character in the Bible, he knows the absence of God. He seeks to solve his problems with his own resources. He experiences the alienating tension imposed by the teaching of the wise. And ultimately in the midst of his aloneness, pain, and sorrow, he discovers a vision of God that transcends all of life. Job's struggle with the absence of God and with the secularist perspective of the world makes this the most relevant book of the Bible for modern man.

Do right and be a success

> My son, do not forget my teaching,
> but guard my commands in your heart;
> for long life and years in plenty
> will they bring you, and prosperity as well.
> Let your good faith and loyalty never fail,

> but bind them about your neck.
> Thus will you win favor and success
> in the sight of God and man
> > [Prov. 3:1–4]

The ethical teaching of the wise men is practical and simple to understand.[4] If one is wise, if he observes life carefully and listens to the instruction of the elders, then he will do what is right, and God will reward him by giving him success. But if one is foolish or lazy, then God will punish him and his misery will be an example for others. There is no escape. This system is ordained by the order found in the universe, which order was established by Wisdom in creation. The wise men have observed it through the ages and that is just the way things are. The total system is based on the common sense motive that being happy is better than being sad and on observation of what actions produce the happy successful life.

A look at some of the proverbs will show how practical the wise men were and how observant they could be of human behavior. These precepts cover all areas of life: one's work, one's relationships with others, and even the kind of attitudes one should have. We shall examine the wise men's teaching under these three headings: work, relationships, and attitudes.

The cardinal virtue of the wise man is hard work. Without it no one can be successful.

> Diligence brings a man to power,
> but laziness to forced labor.
> > [Prov. 12:24]

To be lazy even for just a short time can result in disaster.

A little sleep, a little slumber,
a little folding of the hands in rest,
and poverty will come upon you like a robber,
want like a ruffian.
[Prov. 6:10 ff]

And any excuse one uses to avoid working is of the utmost nonsense.

The sluggard protests,
"There is a lion in the highway,
a lion at large in the streets."
[Prov. 26:13]

While hard work is the primary difference between a rich man and the poor, other factors influence one's success in business. Planning is important; so is style and courage.

Forethought and diligence are sure of profit;
the man in a hurry is as sure of poverty.
[Prov. 21:5]

Be timid in business and come to beggary;
be bold and make a fortune.
[Prov. 11:16*b*]

Care in the selection of employees can mean the difference between a successful business and one that fails.

Like vinegar on the teeth or smoke in the eyes,
so is the lazy servant to his master.
[Prov. 10:26]

> He who sends a fool on an errand
> cuts his own leg off and displays the stump.
> [Prov. 26:6]

In all things, the use of one's wits and intelligence will serve better than dumb brute strength.

> Wisdom prevails over strength,
> Knowledge over brute force;
> for wars are won by skillful strategy,
> and victory is the fruit of long planning.
> [Prov. 24:5 ff]

Honesty is likewise necessary. Although deceitful business practices may produce an immediate profit, they usually result in trouble later.

> Bread got by fraud tastes good,
> but afterwards it fills the mouth with grit.
> [Prov. 20:17]

Work hard, plan ahead, obey the law—then a person will succeed in his life's work. Prosperity will be his.

But there is more to success than just wealth. Having good friends and being respected in the community is likewise of extreme importance. The wise man pays close attention to the establishment and cultivation of good relationships both in the community and in his family. Good relationships with others is not only a sign of success, but also helps him achieve and maintain his well-being.

Aware that one's associates are an important factor in what he does, the wise man avoids bad company and is careful to cultivate positive friendships.

Do not keep company with drunkards
or those who are greedy for the fleshpots;
for drink and greed will end in poverty,
and drunken stupor goes in rags.
[Prov. 23:20 ff]

Never make friends with an angry man
nor keep company with a bad-tempered one;
be careful not to learn his ways,
or you will find yourself caught in a trap.
[Prov. 22:24 ff]

Do not neglect your own friend or your father's;
a neighbor at hand is better than a brother far away.
[Prov. 27:10]

But even among fine, upstanding people, one may easily get entangled in all sorts of problems unless he is careful. Therefore, the wise man does not make too many friends too quickly.

When you make a friend, begin by testing him,
and be in no hurry to trust him.
[Sirach 6:7]

Nor does he take any chances of imposing on their friendship to the point of straining the relationship.

If you find honey, eat only what you need,
too much of it will make you sick;
be sparing in visits to your neighbor's house
if he sees too much of you, he will dislike you.
[Prov. 25:16 ff]

Honesty among friends is essential.

> A straightforward answer
> is as good as a kiss of friendship.
> [Prov. 24:26]

Though at times feelings are best forgotten.

> He who conceals another's offence seeks his goodwill,
> but he who harps on something breaks up friendship.
> [Prov. 17:9]

Above all other things, the wise man will not get into petty disputes with his neighbor—arguing, or gossiping, or witnessing in court against him.

> For lack of fuel a fire dies down
> and for want of a tale-bearer a quarrel subsides.
> [Prov. 26:20]

There is great art in learning to establish and maintain relationships. One must learn when to speak and when to be silent: when to soothe and when to reproach. At times it is best to placate a friend.

> Kind words are like dripping honey,
> sweetness on the tongue and health for the body.
> [Prov. 16:24]

But at other times honesty is what is needed. Certainly honesty is to be preferred over hypocrisy.

> Open reproof is better
> than love concealed.
> [Prov. 27:5]

Glib speech that covers a spiteful heart
is like glaze spread on earthenware.
                    [Prov. 26:23]

If one is to master the art of living, he will do so only by paying close attention to the instruction that is given him, by learning from his mistakes, and by being open to learning from others.

Like a dog returning to its vomit
is a stupid man who repeats his folly.
                    [Prov. 26:11]

As iron sharpens iron,
so one man sharpens the wits of another.
                    [Prov. 27:17]

The worst entanglement of all that a man can fall into, the relationship that has led to the downfall of many an otherwise noble and successful man, is involvement in adultery. Although adultery with a prostitute is truly bad, even worse is an affair with a married woman.

Can a man kindle fire in his bosom
without burning his clothes?
If a man walks on hot coals,
will his feet not be scorched?
So is he who sleeps with his neighbor's wife;
no one can touch such a woman and go free.
. . . .
for a husband's anger is a jealous anger
and in the day of vengeance he will show no mercy.
                    [Prov. 6:27–29, 34]

Happiness for a man is found not with the neighbor's wife, but in the love shared with his own wife.

> Let your fountain, the wife of your youth,
> be blessed, rejoice in her,
> a lovely doe, a graceful hind, let her be
>   your companion;
> you will at all times be bathed in her love.
> [Prov. 5:18 ff]

Carefully cultivated friends, a chaste life, and a good wife—even with these a man's life would be incomplete without children. The wise man's joy is complete only with children and then only if he concerns himself with their education. If brought up correctly by means of instruction and discipline, they will bring honor to their father in his old age. But a child who "runs wild" brings shame on his family (Prov. 29:17, 15).

Wealth, friends, a good wife, and fine children—all these could be lost unless certain attitudes and character traits are developed. The wise men recognized that proper work habits and good relationships simply could not be obtained or maintained unless certain underlying emotional attitudes were cultivated. Thus they also spent time developing the relationship between attitudes and success.

For example, while hard work is good, greed and too much ambition will lead to trouble. Be satisfied with what you make.

> A grasping man brings trouble on his family,
> but he who spurns a bribe will enjoy long life.
> [Prov. 15:27]

The greed that leads one to take a bribe will always get him into trouble, but using money to get out of trouble is simply good sense.

> He who offers a bribe finds it works like a charm,
> he prospers in all he undertakes.
>
> [Prov. 17:8]

In the same way, anger because someone has wronged you will embroil you in a fight and lead to more and more bickering. Remember the order of the world. Those who do wrong will by their very act bring pain upon themselves. Be forgiving and gracious.

> If your enemy is hungry, give him bread to eat;
> if he is thirsty, give him water to drink;
> so you will heap glowing coals on his head,
> and the Lord will reward you.
>
> [Prov. 25:21 ff]

No one enjoys being around a conceited person. Pride and bragging are good ways to offend others. Modesty is a prized personality trait.

> Do not put yourself forward in the king's presence
> or take your place among the great;
> For it is better that he should say to you, "Come
> up here,"
> than move you down to make room for a nobleman.
>
> [Prov. 25:6 ff]

In particular it is difficult for a man to remain modest when he is praised.

The melting-pot is for silver and the crucible for gold,
but praise is the test of character.
[Prov. 27:21]

In all things the wise man will preserve his self control.

Like a city that is breached and left unwalled
is a man who cannot control his temper.
[Prov. 25:28, my translation]

Of course the worst loss of control is by the person who
has had too much wine to drink.

Whose is the misery? whose the remorse?
Whose are the quarrels and the anxiety?
Who gets the bruises without knowing why?
Whose eyes are bloodshot?
Those who linger late over their wine,
those who are always trying some new spiced liquor.
[Prov. 23:29 ff]

Positive thinking is a desirable attitude, for how you
look at life often determines how you will feel.

A merry heart makes a cheerful countenance,
but low spirits sap a man's strength.
[Prov. 17:22]

And finally if a man is to be truly successful, he will be
religious, for the "beginning of wisdom is the fear of the
Lord." To worship God and to be religious is simply one
of the attitudes that is a necessary part of the successful
man's life. Clearly anyone who would ignore the worship
of God would be arrogant, haughty, disrespectful of

tradition and of his elders, and easily tempted to fall into many of the wrong ways.

Now the result if one follows all this advice is that he will have a long life, that he will be wealthy, will be honored in the community, will have a good wife, will have lots of friends and many children who will reward him in his old age with their respect and honor. And if one does not follow this advice, the result is destruction, death, poverty, being despised and spat upon, and having no children, or even worse, having rebellious and troublesome children.

> The blessing of the Lord brings riches,
> and he sends no sorrow with them.
> [Prov. 10:22]

> A poor man is odious even to his friend;
> the rich have friends in plenty.
> [Prov. 14:20]

The whole wisdom way of thinking is based on common sense and observation. The successful life is more desirable than the unsuccessful. If one follows the teaching of the wise men, then he will be successful. The wise men have observed for generations which actions result in success and which acts lead to failure. Their observations provide the basis for action. How could anyone not be motivated to follow in the ways of wisdom and do that which is right!

> Put your neck under *her* yoke,
> let your souls *bear her burden*
> See with your eyes that I have labored little,
> and found for myself much rest.
> [Sirach 51:26 ff, RSV] [5]

How closely the wise men's ethic corresponds to the American value system. We must beware of reading our own standards into the writings of a different culture, but we should not forget that the Puritan work-ethic had its source in the wisdom writings. Honesty, industry, sobriety, thrift, and prudence were the virtues of our forefathers. Like our forefathers we really do believe if we get a good education, do what is right, keep out of trouble, work hard, go to church regularly, marry a good wife (or husband), think positively, and be cheerful and pleasant, then we will be successful. We will have a nice home, well-behaved children, respect in the community, and generally be satisfied with life. Our manner of expressing these beliefs is not the same as that of the wise men—not so poetic nor with as many references to God—but the viewpoints are similar.

This ethic success is on the whole a kind of ethic of prudence. It is not based on a high principle of right and wrong. There is no concept here of equal justice for all men. The moral tone that we find in the law or the prophets is simply not to be found in Proverbs. Instead, the basis of this ethic is the observation of how one gets ahead in life. To read the Book of Proverbs is to take a fourth-century B.C. Dale Carnegie course. Learn the right techniques and you will be happy and successful. If you think positively, learn a few skills for relating to others, work hard, and lead a basically moral life (only bribing when necessary); then you are going to be successful.

The emphasis in Proverbs on the proper training of youth suggests that youth in ancient Israel, like youth today, did not embrace the wisdom teaching unhesitatingly. The preceding synopsis of the wisdom ethic has stressed the self-evident nature of the wise men's observations, but to the untrained mind the obvious is not always so clear. In the face of the endless variability of human situations and in view of man's propensity for self-delusion, only experience can recognize the true consequences of an action.

> A road may seem straightforward to a man,
> yet may end as a way to death.
> [Proverbs 14:12]

To fully recognize the relationship between act and consequence requires astute observation and a lifetime of experience. The greatest safeguard against taking the wrong path was the durability of the proverbs through generations of observation (Prov. 4:1–5). The elders alone had lived long enough to distinguish with certainty the good from the evil, and often that knowledge had to be beaten into the students (13:24; 22:15; 23:13 ff; 29:15).

Surely part of the problem in motivating the youth lay in the nature of ethical action. The reward for right action (i.e., success) frequently seems distant, but the cost (e.g., hard work) is immediate. On the other hand, the reward for immoral or dishonest action is immediate, while the undesirable consequences appear distant and avoidable. The wise men could not shorten the time span between action and reward, but they could and did absolutize the relationship between action and consequence. If one acted rightly, he would reap the rewards of success. If one acted wrongly, he would be punished with failure.

In Proverbs there is no exception to this understanding of retribution—namely, that God through the world's structure rewards the good and punishes the bad. If a man is poor it is because he is lazy (12:11, 24; 13:4; 18:9; 19:15; 20:4, 13; 22:7; 24:34) or immoral (13:25) or has failed to listen to instruction and plan his life (13:18; 21:5) or loves pleasure too much (21:17) or all of the above. Over and over we find this theme of retribution reiterated.

> Ill fortune follows the sinner close behind,
> but good rewards the righteous.
> > [Prov. 13:21]

Anyone who looks at the world recognizes that there are good men who know pain and evil men who are successful. The wise men were observers. They too saw the success of wicked men and the sufferings of the righteous. But these apparent contradictions of retribution did not shake the orthodox in their faith. The wise men explained away the apparent contradictions through two basic arguments.

The first explanation centered on the inability of a man to know all about another person. God alone knows a man's heart and rewards or punishes him for his true spirit, not just his outward appearance.

> A man's whole conduct may be pure in his own eyes,
> but the Lord fixes a standard for the spirit of man.
> > [Prov. 16:2]

The second explanation focused on the time-lag before the rewards or punishments become effective. One day's hard work does not produce a rich man. This delay is what makes instruction necessary. A person must be motivated to continue in the right even though the wicked man seems to be prospering with less work, for in the end justice will prevail.[6]

> The wicked man is caught in his own iniquities
> and held fast in the toils of his own sin;

he will perish for want of discipline,
gripped in the shroud of his boundless folly.
[Prov. 5:22 ff]

Just as a teacher must sometimes discipline a student, so
God tests the righteous with hard times.

My son, do not spurn the Lord's correction
or take offence at his reproof;
for those whom he loves the Lord reproves,
and he punishes a favorite son.
[Prov. 3:11 ff]

But ultimately the good man always triumphs.

Though the good man may fall seven times,
he is soon up again,
but the rascal is brought down by misfortune.
[Prov. 24:16]

One might expect that so absolute a doctrine of
retribution would encourage some of the wise men to
reverse the relationship between moral goodness and
prosperity. If a man is prosperous, then he must be so
because God has rewarded his moral character. The poor,
the sick, and the suffering, on the other hand, are being
punished by God. This converse of retribution could easily
become an excuse for inhumanity to the weak and helpless
and for judgmental condemnation of the dispossessed.
Though there is no such reversal in Proverbs, apparently
such judgment of the poor and the sick was not uncom-
mon as we see in many of the psalms.

O God of my praise, be silent no longer,
for wicked men heap calumnies upon me.

They have lied to my face
  and ringed me round with words of hate.
They have attacked me without a cause
  and accused me though I have done nothing unseemly.

. . . .

for I am downtrodden and poor,
  and my heart within me is distracted.

. . . .

My knees are weak with fasting,
  and my flesh wastes away, so meagre is my fare.
I have become the victim of their taunts,
  when they see me they toss their heads.

               [Ps. 109:1–4, 22, 24 ff] [7]

The wise men's ethic of success was tempered by three factors. The first tempering factor was the law of the Lord given to Moses and handed down to his people. Wisdom did not exist in a vacuum; it was balanced by Mosaic law and the prophetic call to righteousness. Even kings had to obey the Torah. There is some identity of moral concern in both the Torah and wisdom. For example, before there were surveyors or maps, boundaries were marked by stones and other natural objects. How easily one could increase his estate by moving a boundary marker. In Proverbs we find strong admonition against such an action.

    Do not move the ancient boundary-stone
    or encroach on the lands of orphans:
    they have a powerful guardian
    who will take up their cause against you.
               [Prov. 23:10 ff]

This same ethic principle is found in the law of Moses (Deut. 19:14; 27:17). Similarly we find the prophetic concern for just business dealings proverbialized:

> A double standard in weights is an abomination to
>   the Lord,
> And false scales are not good in his sight.
> [Prov. 20:23]

Even greater altruistic and ethical concern is expressed in the sentences urging impartiality in the dispensing of justice.

> A judge who pronounces a guilty man innocent
> is cursed by all nations, all peoples execrate him;
> but for those who convict the guilty all will go well,
> they will be blessed with prosperity.
> [Prov. 24:24 ff]

And in sentences which implore compassionate action toward the poor.

> He who oppresses the poor insults his Maker;
> he who is generous to the needy honors him.
> [Prov. 14:31]

A second mitigation of the wise men's ethic was the realization that the materially successful life alone is not always true success. Being happy and at peace is also important. If one should have to choose between wealth and happiness, clearly happiness is preferable.

> Better to live in a corner of the house-top
> than have a nagging wife and a brawling household.
> [Prov. 25:24]

Better a dish of vegetables if love go with it,
than a fat ox eaten in hatred.

[Prov. 15:17]

In Job we shall see that when the ideal wise man (Job) has
lost everything, what he prized most and grieved over
longest was his honor and esteem in the community (Job
30). Honor as the highest good is suggested in Proverbs
(22:1) and is expressed directly in Sirach.

The days of a good life are numbered,
but a good name lasts for ever.

[Sirach 41:13]

The final moderating influence was the limitation of
human knowledge and understanding. The wise man
studies all that is possible; he may plan carefully; he may
try to do what is right; but there is still the possibility that
life can go against him; he may still make mistakes.

A man may spend freely and yet grow richer;
another is sparing beyond measure, yet ends
in poverty.

[Prov. 11:24]

Even in laughter the heart may grieve,
and mirth may end in sorrow.

[Prov. 14:13]

This inability to know the future may have its good side
also.

Like cold water to the throat when it is dry
is good news from a distant land.
> [Prov. 25:25]

Home and wealth may come down from the ancestors,
but an intelligent wife is a gift from the Lord.
> [Prov. 19:14]

In all things it is wise to be modest, humble, and to live in
the fear of the Lord. The greatest folly is to believe one is
the master of his life.

It is plain stupidity to trust in one's own wits,
but he who walks the path of wisdom will come safely
through.
> [Prov. 28:26]

Job, the rebel

Job is the perfect man. He is righteous in every detail:
scrupulous in his observance of moral and religious laws,
compassionate toward the poor and the orphaned, pure in
thought, and sincerely pious in his worship. Job is the ideal
wise man. Even God attests to his rectitude (Job 1 and 31).

Yet tragic loss after tragic loss strips Job of his children,
his wealth, his prestige, and his health. The wise men's
mechanistic view of retribution does not hold up! Job is
the fictional example, but he reflects the reality: innocent
men do suffer. Job sits with the afflicted—a startling
contradiction to the wise men's faith in retribution.

There is a popular idea that the Book of Job attempts to
answer the question of why the innocent suffer. In Job's
time, however, this simply was not a problem. The wise
men were firm in their belief: The innocent did not suffer.
If a person suffered, it was because he was evil. Or if a

good man suffered, it was only temporary—a test of his goodness. He would soon be prosperous. Job was not written to answer the question of why the innocent suffer. Job was written to affirm the fact that the innocent do suffer! Job was written in revolt against the orthodoxy that saw all suffering as justified.

Since the Elihu speeches (Job 32–37) are not by the author of Job but are by someone who lived at about the same time, they give us the reaction of a contemporary author. These speeches confirm for us that a basic intent of the Book of Job is to affirm that the innocent do suffer. Elihu's author saw clearly that in spite of the divine speeches at the end and in spite of the epilogue, the conclusion stood—Job, the innocent man, suffered great pain. He was neither convicted by the friends nor by God (32:12). This is the reason Elihu spends as much time *accusing Job* of sin as he does trying to explain the reasons for suffering. The author of Elihu's speeches understood the point of the book completely. He understood that Job, the wretched sufferer, claimed to be morally innocent (33:8–11; 34:5–6; 35:2–3). He even understood the implication of Job's suffering, namely that wealth and righteousness are unrelated (34:17–30). And he frantically reaffirmed orthodox wisdom.

Job was not written to justify the ways of God to man. Job is not the defender of the faith; Job is the defender of the suffering and the helpless against the unjust accusations of wisdom's theology. Job is the perfect man to make it absolutely clear that the *innocent* do suffer. He is denying that the poor, the sick, and the oppressed are in their positions as punishment for immorality. The author was so successful in affirming that the innocent do suffer, that from his time forward men have accepted that conclusion and have been concerned to understand why it is so.

CHAPTER 2

THE DRAMA BEGINS

Why was I not still-born,
why did I not die when I came out of the womb?
[Job 3:11]

Do you mean to argue about words
or to sift the utterance of a man past hope?
Would you assail an orphan?
Would you hurl yourselves on a friend?
[Job 6:26 ff]

My mind is distraught, my days are numbered,
and the grave is waiting for me.
Wherever I turn, men taunt me,
and my day is darkened by their sneers.
[Job 17:1 ff]

The emotional tension expressed throughout the Book of
Job is created by the opening account of Job's losses.
Bereft of health, children, wealth, and prestige, Job is
hardly in a frame of mind for a dispassionate investigation
into the ways of God. Job is a man trying to survive,
seeking comfort from his friends and support from God.
With outbursts of anger and of protest, Job cries out for
help. Failing to receive help or to find answers to his

questions, he sinks into the depths of despair. The drama
of Job is an empathetic portrayal of human despair and
suffering.

How different this emotional barrage is from the quiet,
reflective study of life found in the wise men's proverbs!
But Job is written by one of the wise men, and the contrast
between the impassioned Book of Job and the dispassionate teaching of the wise is simply one reflection of the
author's rebellion against the staid orthodoxy of his day.
Job, the perfect man, yet a by-word for suffering and
failure, stands as a stark contradiction to the wisdom
doctrine of retribution. What good is the wise men's
advice about work, family, and friends to Job? What good
is the God known only through observation of the orderly
workings of the world to the man whose world is in chaos?

The poet of life

Who is the author of the Book of Job? What do we
know about this rebel who paints such a dark picture on
the bright collage of optimistic wisdom? When and where
did he live?

We do not know the author's name. All we know about
him is deduced from his writing. While the prose story that
frames the poetic dialogue is set in the patriarchal period,
the majority of critics date the composition of the poetry,
primarily on the basis of vocabulary, in the period
following the Babylonian exile. There is no indication in
the text of a particular setting. We must be satisfied with
the broad range in date of 550–200 B.C. The strong
monotheism, the concern for the individual, and the fact
that this book represents the highest development of
Hebrew wisdom all support a late date.

The author was a highly educated member of the

intelligentsia writing for a cosmopolitan audience. The language of the Book of Job is the most abstruse Hebrew in the Bible. Job is a very literary work. We are limited in knowing the Hebrew language because Job is the only truly erudite book we have. Translating Job is analogous to trying to read Shakespeare if you did not know English and your only source for learning it was the daily newspaper. The difficulty of language is compounded by many corrupt and unintelligible portions in the received Hebrew text.

In viewpoint the Book of Job is international to the point of being almost non-Hebraic. There are no references to Israel, the land, its history, its culture, or its religion (with the exception of the use of the divine name, Yahweh, in the prologue, epilogue, and superscription of the divine speeches). The civil and moral prescriptions alluded to have an international character. The author's moral standards as delineated in chapter 31 are far in advance of his contemporaries whether he be Judean or not. The lack of nationalistic references is further complicated by hints of a foreign background. The names of Job and his three friends are non-Hebraic. The descriptions of Behemoth (the hippopotamus) and Leviathan (the crocodile) and the reference to ships of papyrus (9:26) point to Egyptian sources. Some commentators have even suggested that the author was not Hebrew. I believe that the faith expressed in the Book of Job and the picture drawn of God reflect the depth of the Jewish faith. The international character is an expression of the cosmopolitan, upperclass orientation of wisdom literature. Perhaps the author was well traveled. He was certainly well versed in the lore of the ancient Near East.

The poet had a fervent desire to know the truth. He bluntly presented the situation of a suffering man to a philosophy oriented around success. Through that situation he challenged the accepted explanation of suffering, the value of success, and the prevailing conception of God. Surely the ardent speeches of Job express the impassioned search of the poet for truth. Seeing people suffer and how society treated them, the author of Job used the suffering of the innocent Job to challenge the orthodox dogma of divine retribution with a passionate concern for truth and a compassionate defense of the sufferer.

A third characteristic of the author makes the book a classic. He was a deeply religious man, sensitive to the suffering of humanity and of individuals. His sensitivity may have come through personal trials. Even if he did not suffer physically, however, one can safely assume he suffered out of empathy and sympathy for others. Many authors have dramatically portrayed human suffering. Only the great have equaled the author of Job in tracing the psychological destruction that accompanies great pain. But none have seen human suffering so clearly and at the same time seen so powerful a vision of God! In fact, few works of literature have ever been able to draw the picture of God successfully. (For example, in Milton's *Paradise Lost* Satan is a much stronger character than God.) But the author of Job is able to see and to portray the God who is God as well as a man who is every man.

The lack of a particular setting in time or place, the wide range of subject matter, the literary skill of the author, the writer's concern for truth, his sensitivity to the human situation, and his depth of faith together combine to make Job a work for all times.

The man of faith

(Suggested reading, Job 1:1–2:10; 42:10–17. As mentioned in the preface, at various points throughout this volume, readings in Job will be suggested. These readings will allow the reader to read through Job in conjunction with this essay.)

Jewish and Christian tradition have created a popular misconception that at the time of his trials Job is a man of advanced years. There is not the slightest basis for this impression in either the prose or the poetry. Job is struck down in the prime of life. His children are not married, and in a culture practicing early marriage that places Job under forty. At the end of the story Job is still vigorous enough to beget a large family. In the dialogue Job's young age is also indicated. That the aged stood up when Job entered is significant only if Job is younger (29:7ff). Claiming to be on the side of men older than Job's father, Eliphaz condemns Job's youthfulness (15:9ff). Finally, Job's energetic and obstinate speeches are more appropriate for a man in his prime than for one whose life is largely spent.

There lived in the land of Uz a man of blameless and upright life named Job, who feared God and set his face against wrongdoing. [Job 1:1]

Even if those three men were living there—Noah, Daniel, and Job, they would save none but themselves by their righteousness. [Ezek. 14:14]

Job, the ideal man, famous for his rectitude and piety, was a man of wealth and the father of a large and happy family. Then all changes. In one day he loses all he had—sons, daughters, slaves, and cattle. A loathsome disease, marked by swellings and ulcers, covers his whole body. His reputation gone, we now behold him seated in ashes, scraping himself with a broken piece of pottery to try to relieve his illness. What is Job's response to this change of fortune? Does he submit passively saying only, "If we accept good from God, shall we not accept evil?" (2:10). Or does he cry out, "I loath my life; I will give free utterance to my complaint; I will speak in the bitterness of my soul" (10:1)?

"The patience of Job" is another widespread misconception. This time the distortion originates in the book itself. The prose prologue gives one response Job makes to his suffering; the poetic dialogue portrays the opposite. The difference in the picture of Job is only one of many conflicts between the prose frame story and the poetic dialogue. If we take the prose prologue (1:1–2:13) and the epilogue (42:7–17) together, we find an essentially consistent and self-contained narrative of the testing of a patient and pious man. Throughout this narrative Job is clearly innocent of any possible crime or blasphemy. In the end he is restored to his former position. In the poetry Job is a doubter, a violent rebel, a proud giant, and a challenger of God. In the end he repents. In the narrative frame Job is portrayed as a nomad and owner of flocks and herds (1:3) spread over a vast area (1:13–17), while in the poetic discourse he is a tiller of soil (31:1, 12, 24, 34, 38–40) and is respected by the elders of a city (29:7) where he appears to dwell (19:15). In the prose narrative Job pays scrupulous attention to observing the requirements of the sacrificial cultus (1:5; 42:8); in the poem such observances are unmentioned by either Job or the friends.

Differences are also found in areas other than the portrait of Job. The evil in the prose results from a divine wager between God and the satan, the adversary.[1] In the poetry no possible cause for suffering is mentioned other than God's righteous punishment of sin. The artificial vindication of Job and restoration of his family and goods (as if that would solve anything) directly contradicts the cry of the poetry that one cannot count on such treatment.

There are stylistic differences as well. The difference between prose and poetry explains some changes in style, but the detached view of suffering expressed in the prologue differs fundamentally from the realistic and anguished cries of the tormented Job of the dialogue. Vocabulary differences are most vividly illustrated by the use of divine names. The prose uses only the names Yahweh and Elohim, the common Hebrew words. The poetry uses the more abstract words for God: El, Eloah, Elohim, and Shaddai and avoids the personal Yahweh.

Taken together these factors indicate that the prose frame derives from an independent narrative about a hero of the faith connected by Ezekiel with Noah and Daniel (Ezek. 14:14-20). The literary structure contains the elements of repetition and schematization associated with folk tales. The conclusion is generally held now that the prose frame is an ancient folk tale told to illustrate the proverb: "Though the good man may fall seven times, he is soon up again; but the rascal is brought down by misfortune" (Prov. 24:16).[2] It is, of course, to this folk tale that Ezekiel refers and not our canonical Book of Job.

Whether this tale came to the author of Job as oral tradition or in written form is largely an academic question. In either case the details present in the tale were fixed. The implication is clear: we no longer have to assume that the author intended *every* detail of the prose to be included in the understanding of Job and his situation. But the conclusion is not so clear: which details does the author intend for us to remember as we read the dialogue? And are all the details of the prose determined by the folk tale, or did our author add some when he adapted the frame to his poetry?

The first step in answering these two questions is to

determine what was the original story. Some have proposed that the original folk tale was longer than our present prose and that it contained a different form of counsel from the friends. The simplest and best understanding is that the author took the folk tale in its entirety and added the three friends. The original tale is 1:1–2:10 and 42:10–17. This forms a very clear, concise story of the testing of Job. It reads smoothly[3] and is self-evident in meaning. Job is the man of faith held up as an example for all men. A person, according to this story, should endure pain patiently and in quiet resignation. He must not swerve from the line of righteous conduct simply because life is hard. This simple, straight-forward folk tale has a great impact. In fact the impact is so strong that, in spite of chapters 3–41, Job has been consistently interpreted (wrongly) in both Jewish and Christian piety as a man of patience (e.g., James 5:11).

Certain elements of this folk tale then were fixed by tradition. Some of these may not have been intended as a part of the author's meaning. Through Job, the poet portrayed the suffering of an innocent man. But nowhere in the poetry does he explain why an innocent man would suffer. That he chose the tale of Job to explain suffering as the result of divine pride in a man's integrity is unlikely in the extreme. The divine speeches at the end of the dialogue make it clear that God is much too great to get involved in a little bit of petty gambling. Nor is the satan an explanation of suffering. God has total control. The satan can only act as God gives him permission. We may safely reject the implications of the ending with its double portions of sheep, camels, oxen, and she-asses. While the ending may serve as a second vindication of Job, in no way does it answer the question of why the innocent suffer. Job still suffers unjustly, even if everything does come out all right in the end. The folk tale is not about suffering; it is about a man passing a test, the success of righteousness. The author was an intelligent man. We may safely assume he did not intend for us to examine the folk tale as an explanation for the evil done to Job.

On the other hand, we may regard the condemnation of the friends (42:7, 8) as a detail written by and desired by the poet. His motive is clear. Job has just been confronted by God and has just repented, saying, "Therefore I despise myself: I repent in dust and ashes." Was this not what the friends had been telling him to do all along? If the poet had ended the story here with only the restoration of Job, then the friends and their viewpoint would have been vindicated, not Job. The work would lose much of its impact if at the end one were not certain that Job was right. God's rebuke of the friends is an essential part for our understanding of the book.

We now come to the central question regarding the folk tale. Why did the author pick the story of Job as the medium for his message? What was communicated to his readers by that well-known tale? What was the essential meaning of the Job story that motivated the author to use it as a theme for his work? Clearly, the main point of the tale is not to explain the existence of evil in the world. The whole thrust of the story is to describe the nature of genuine piety and authentic devotion. The figure of the satan is irrelevant in an explanation for suffering, but his question defines the point of the story, "Has not Job good reason to be God-fearing? . . . Strike him and all that he has and he will curse you to your face" (1:9, 11). The question raised by the story is the question of why we worship God. Do we fear him that we might receive rewards? Or do we really love God for the sake of God alone? Job was put to that test. And in passing the test he becomes the example of true selfless devotion for all men. Job is, above all else, the man of faith.

Understood in this light the story of Job adds a new dimension to the previously stated concern of the author for countering orthodox wisdom's mechanistic view of retribution. As a defender of the sick, the poor, and the downcast against unjust judgment, he affirms that the innocent do suffer. Suffering does not imply guilt. The story of the suffering, innocent Job was an obvious illustration of what he wanted to say. But the destruction of the theology of retribution raises anew the problem of faith in God. Orthodox wisdom had good motive to worship God—it would result in a successful life. But if the righteous suffer, then why have faith? What good is faith? Job was the innocent sufferer; he was also the man of faith. In choosing the tale of Job, the author promises us he will be concerned with more than defense of the downcast. He tells us he will also explore the nature of true faith—faith that is not a bribe for a reward, but faith that believes and cares for God simply because God is.

The opening scene
(suggested reading, Job 3–5)

"For seven days and seven nights they sat beside him on the ground, and none of them said a word to him; for they saw that his suffering was very great" (2:13). This one sentence conveys to the reader succinctly and dramatically the great suffering of Job. Then Job breaks the silence with one of the most poignant laments ever written. He begins by cursing the day of his birth (3:3–10). His words are addressed neither to his friends nor to God. He simply cries out in pain.

> Perish the day when I was born
> and the night which said, "A man is conceived"!

He follows this curse by lamenting his survival. Since he was born, why did he not die at birth and enter Sheol where at least he would know no pain (3:11–19)? Finally he expresses his personal pain on a more philosophical level (3:20–23).

> Why should the sufferer be born to see the light?
> Why is life given to men who find it so bitter?

The image of a patient and submissive Job has been shattered. In verse 23 he parodies the prologue when he says,

> Why should a man be born to wander blindly,
> hedged in by God on every side?

In the prose God's protection and compensation were described in similar words (1:10). Suddenly being hedged in by God is the most awful experience possible. It brings the pain and suffering Job is experiencing.

This expression of Job's despair is alone a masterpiece of writing. It is on par with other classic speeches of despair—Cassandra in *Trojan Women* or Ophelia in *Hamlet*. Job cries out in sheer pain. The pain is that felt by anyone at the loss of a wife or husband or child. Like any bereaved person Job is in effect saying, "What is there to live for? If only I too could die! Why go on!" This is not (for the bereaved nor for Job) a suicide wish: there is no thought of ending his life. He cries out, not to threaten suicide, but to give vent to the crushing pain and despair. His sorrow compels his cry.

Eliphaz responds with these words of comfort:

> If one ventures to speak with you, will you lose
>   patience?
> For who could hold his tongue any longer?

Think how once you encouraged those who faltered,
how you braced feeble arms,
how a word from you upheld the stumblers
and put strength into weak knees.
But now that adversity comes upon you, you lose
        patience:
it touches you, and you are unmanned.
Is your religion no comfort to you?
Does your blameless life give you no hope?
For consider, what innocent man has ever perished?
Where have you seen the upright destroyed?
This I know, that those who plough mischief and
        sow trouble
reap as they have sown;
they perish at the blast of God
and are shrivelled by the breath of his nostrils.

[4:2–9]

What a strange response this seems to be! As we look back
twenty-two centuries, we wonder how a friend could say
anything like that. But what should one say to Job? From
a twentieth-century, Christian viewpoint, what would one
say to someone, a friend, who has recently had great loss
in his life, and who is bewailing his lot with cries that he
would like to die? Would the comfort of the modern,
faithful Christian really be that different from the kind of
consolation Eliphaz offers? Eliphaz and the friends are the
solid, orthodox churchmen of their day. One type of
response people make today goes something like this: "Oh,
don't talk like that! Everything is going to be all right.
Believe me. God will see you through. Have faith; it will
be all right." That is precisely the response Eliphaz had
made, only in a different idiom. He was very gentle with
Job. "Come on," he said, "have faith. I have heard you
give people great encouragement. You are a man of great

faith. We all know that. Come on now, put it to work. If you'll just have faith, it'll all be O.K."

Of course the description of faith from Eliphaz is different from ours. Eliphaz is a wise man. As we have seen, a basic tenet of the wise man's faith is that God will reward the righteous and punish the wicked. Eliphaz encourages Job on the basis of that faith to think positively, because after all Job's life has been blameless (4:6). Esoteric dreams are the only way the rationalistic wise men come into personal contact with God. On the basis of such a nocturnal revelation by an apparition, Eliphaz seeks to reconcile Job's innocence with his suffering. All men, he says, are imperfect in the eyes of God. Therefore Job should not lose faith or patience (4:12–5:2). Then emphasizing God's care for the righteous (only a few verses of the two chapters mention the fall of the wicked), Eliphaz encourages Job to pray to God, the savior of the just (5:8–26).

> For my part, I would make my petition to God
> and lay my cause before him,
> who does great and unsearchable things,
> marvels without number.
>
> . . . .
>
> He saves the destitute from their greed,
> and the needy from the grip of the strong;
> so the poor hope again,
> and the unjust are sickened.
>
> . . . .
>
> For, though he wounds, he will bind up;
> the hands that smite will heal.
> You may meet disaster six times, and he will save you;
> seven times, and no harm shall touch you.
>
> [5:8 ff, 15 ff, 18 ff] [4]

It is easy for us to see the judgment implied in Eliphaz's comfort. If God rewards goodness and punishes wickedness, then even though Eliphaz called Job innocent, by implication God must be punishing him for something evil that he has done. The very nature of the wise man's faith implied sinfulness to anyone who had a tragedy in his life. It is more difficult for us to see the judgment implied in our comforting. Yet to encourage people to have faith is to imply that if they had faith enough they would be cured of their illness or they would not have this tragedy. Many a Christian has been told or has said that very thought. What is communicated is the judgment that one is ill, lonely, or depressed because he lacks faith. In other words, he is bad and God is punishing him. Hidden just below the surface of our own consolation, like that of Eliphaz, is a strong judgmental statement against the very person we would comfort.

I believe the basic reason for the similarity is that we like Eliphaz come out of a success-oriented culture. We cannot deal with despair, failure, or even illness. We want everyone to be happy and cheerful and successful. We want to solve all our problems, and long term illness or deep despair, if they are solvable, are not solved easily or quickly. So we tell the person who is ill to cheer up, think positively, pray, be happy. And then we get away as fast as possible. No one enjoys being with people who are unhappy, but surely it is our success orientation that makes it so difficult for us. By their very being they remind us that success is an illusion, that it is not under our own control or really a result of our own efforts.

Our success-oriented culture deals with failure just like the wise men. We categorize and judge it making it the individual's own fault, thereby removing ourselves from such distress. "The poor are poor because they don't work hard enough." "The man's business failed because he did not plan well enough." "That person is a hypochondriac; he could be well if he really wanted to be." The function of such statements is not to state great truths. Rather they are designed to assign guilt for failure and unhappiness. When the American dream becomes nightmarish, we want to blame someone, someone else. Even when such statements do contain some truth, their purpose is not to investigate reality but to assign guilt, to separate us from the outcasts, and to protect us from seeing our brother in need.

I am convinced that the best thing Eliphaz and the friends could have done would have been to continue sitting quietly. All would have been well had they simply been with Job in a quiet, accepting manner, a ministry of presence. Consolation almost always contains within it a judgment. In sitting quietly with the friend in need, in accepting his powerlessness to change the world, in sharing in his lack of knowing why, one may minister to his friend simply by his presence. True ministry to those who suffer is always to share in their suffering by being with them. I have often seen a child be the best minister to a parent or grandparent who is bereaved. The child does not know words of consolation. He knows no doctrines of the faith we offer as help. He spontaneously ministers simply by his presence.

This is the kind of ministry exemplified by Jesus. Even though the story is overlaid with a theological framework, we can see Jesus ministering with this depth of sharing at the death of his friend Lazarus. He did not come to Mary and Martha and say, "If you had had more faith this would not have happened." He did not even say "Cheer up, everything will be all right." He came with a ministry of presence. He came to the tomb and he wept. He broke down and cried. Love so ministers. He shared in Mary and

Martha's pain. It was the power of that love that raised Lazarus.

All of us who seek to minister to others need constantly to evaluate our own lives and our own responses to despair and failure. Any true ministry to the outcast, the poor, or the ill is not advice from outside, but empathy from alongside. It is not judgment from above, but quiet acceptance. It is not analysis of the situation, but presence within the situation beside the one in need.

CHAPTER 3

JOB AND HIS FRIENDS

(suggested reading, Job 6–15)

JOB: Every terror that haunted me has caught up
with me,
and all that I feared has come upon me.
There is no peace of mind nor quiet for me;
I chafe in torment and have no rest.

[3:25 ff]

ELIPHAZ: Happy the man whom God rebukes!
Therefore do not reject the discipline
of the Almighty.
For, though he wounds, he will bind up;
the hands that smite will heal.

[5:17 ff]

Job cries out in pain and despair. Eliphaz, believing his
friend to be a moral and religious man, attempts to
comfort Job with the doctrines of religious belief. Totally
unable to deal with Job's despair, Eliphaz retreats into the
more comfortable, insulated area of creedal faith. Incapa-
ble of helping Job and perhaps fearful that his own faith
might be shaken, Eliphaz urges Job to affirm his orthodoxy by humbly praying to God and patiently trusting

God to reward him with the good life again. Job did not ask a religious or philosophical question. He only cried out in pain. But Eliphaz responded with a theological discourse. They are speaking on totally different levels: Job is on an emotional level; Eliphaz, on a philosophical; and there is no true communication between them. This lack of communication makes the dialogue appear disjointed, even though they interact strongly.

Job's initial reaction to Eliphaz's "comfort" is an attempt to be understood.

> Does the wild ass bray when he has grass
> or the ox low when he has fodder?
>
> [6:5]

"It should be simple to you," Job is saying. "I hurt. That is why I cry out in pain. If there were no pain, I would not cry out. I am not concerned with theology."

Then in a subtle twisting of Eliphaz's advice to pray and hope, Job calls upon God to grant his request for a speedy death (6:8 ff). It is death that will bring him relief, not hope in a distant future (6:10).

Job clearly picked up the implied judgment in his friend's "consolation." He now for the first time becomes concerned about his character evaluation. The desire for death takes on a new dimension: death becomes a way of preserving his integrity (6:10c, NEB, footnote). Until this point in his life he has been an innocent man, but in the face of such suffering (6:11 ff) and lack of support from his friends (6:13), he fears he might sin. Immediate death would insure that he had run his life's course righteously.

Having poured out his soul again, Job somehow knows that his friends do not understand. He feels the lack of communication and the accompanying judgment. He gives up trying to share himself and turns toward them in anger.

> Devotion is due from his friends
> to one who despairs and loses faith in the Almighty;
> but my brothers have been treacherous as a mountain
>   stream,
> like the channels of streams that run dry,
> which turn dark with *thawing ice*
> *and are filled with melted snow,*
> *when it warms they fade,*
> dwindle in the heat and are gone.
> Then the caravans, winding hither and thither,
> go up into the wilderness and perish.
> . . . .
> So treacherous have you now been to me:
> you felt dismay and were afraid.
>
> [6:14–18,21] [1]

Job can see his friends are threatened by him; his pain makes them afraid. Perhaps their inability to understand, perhaps the arrogance of a pat answer to deep sorrow, perhaps the recognition that his friends are repulsed and afraid of him—something makes Job suddenly turn on all his friends and in bitter sarcasm cry out:

> Tell me plainly, and I will listen in silence;
> show me where I have erred.
> How harsh are the words of the upright man!
> What do the arguments of wise men prove?
> Do you mean to argue about words
> or to sift the utterance of a man past hope?
> Would you assail an orphan?
> Would you hurl yourselves on a friend?

> So now, I beg you, turn and look at me:
> am I likely to lie to your faces?
> Think again, let me have no more injustice;
> think again, for my integrity is in question.
>
> [6:24–29]

Job has heard the implied judgment. He sees the accusation within Eliphaz's advice. In anger he asks his friends to show him where he has sinned. Berating them for the harshness of their theology, he begs them not to treat him unjustly. Job's concern for his integrity, hinted at briefly above (6:10c), is beginning to grow in the face of the friends' admonitions.

He then paints a moving picture of his physical and mental anguish, all of which is more difficult to bear because life is fleeting and there is little time for hope (7:1–6).

> So months of futility are my portion,
> troubled nights are my lot.
> When I lie down, I think,
> "When will it be day that I may rise?"
> When the evening grows long and I lie down,
> I do nothing but toss till morning twilight.
> My body is infested with worms,
> and scabs cover my skin.
> My days are swifter than a shuttle
> and come to an end as the thread runs out.
>
> [7:3–6]

The torments of the night (here and in 3:13 ff) take on special significance in the wise men's perspective. The only personal contact one has with the abstract God is through dreams. Job's nocturnal torment is one factor leading him to see God as an oppressive enemy (7:13–16).

In the face of the friends' judgment and lack of understanding, Job turns to God. In an angry prayer he closes this speech by asking God to get off his back (7:7–21). A person's relationship with God is influenced by and influences his relationship with others. So Job's interaction with his friends affects his relationship with God. Though we are looking at these two relationships separately, Job's responses to the friends are intertwined with his prayers to God throughout the dialogue.

Job's speech in these two chapters not only presents a good picture of Job's suffering, but also illustrates the literary skill of the author. Blending together sarcasm, pathos, pleading, accusation, and anger, Job tells his friends what it is like to be in his situation. This beautifully written speech clearly expresses how Job feels; but the friends are unable to hear what he is saying.

Bildad is neither sympathetic nor empathetic. Threatened by the innocent sufferer and in reaction to Job's anger, he moves directly to the judgmental, philosophical point.

> How long will you say such things,
> the long-winded ramblings of an old man?
> Does God pervert judgment?
> Does the Almighty pervert justice?
>
> [8:2 ff]

Concerned with his religious beliefs, Bildad could not hear the cry of pain. All he could hear was an accusation that God is unjust. Job of course has not said anything about the justice of God. He has asked only that his friends not misjudge him. His claim of innocence was not arrogant.

He decried the friends' false judgment, but asked God to ignore or remove what guilt he has (7:20 ff). It is their defensiveness that makes Job's friends hear his claim of innocence as an attack against God.

Though less sympathetic, Bildad like Eliphaz is still seeking to console Job. After suggesting that perhaps Job's sons had sinned, he appeals to the experience of the ancestors in an exposition of orthodox wisdom (chap. 8). God rewards the just and punishes the wicked. Seek God, and *if* you are innocent he will make your past as nothing in comparison with your new prosperity. Bildad makes no accusation that Job is evil. He still seems to assume that Job is just and God will see him through.

> Be sure, God will not spurn the blameless man,
> nor will he grasp the hand of the wrongdoer,
> He will yet fill your mouth with laughter,
> and shouts of joy will be on your lips;
> [8:20 ff]

In response to Bildad's philosophical discourse, Job turns toward God (chaps. 9 and 10). The exposition of orthodox wisdom in response to Job's anger and pathos is a clear denial of either Job's innocence or his pain. But of equal or greater importance, Bildad's bantering is a rejection of Job's cries for support. Recognizing this total lack of communication, Job wonders if he might be able to confront God. Job too believes orthodox wisdom and accepts its view of retribution. Both Eliphaz and Bildad have suggested that he pray to God. Perhaps if he could encounter God, then God would show the friends he was an innocent man. The friends expect Job to turn to God and, repenting for some unknown sin, to beg humbly for forgiveness and restitution. But Job does not consider repentance. He turns toward God and speculates on how he might prevail upon God to restore him because of his innocence.

> I will speak out in bitterness of soul.
> I will say to God, "Do not condemn me,
> but tell me the ground of thy complaint against me.
> Dost thou find any advantage in oppression,
> in spurning the fruit of all thy labor?
> . . . .
> Thou knowest that I am guiltless
> and have none to save me from thee?"
>
> [10:1c–3b, 7]

Zophar responds quickly (chap. 11) to Job's unusual petition. Job has said he would like to confront God. Zophar immediately gives his view of what such a confrontation would be like (11:4–6). If God would speak, *11:4–6* he would expound to Job the secrets of wisdom, and he would know that God exacts from him less than his sin deserves. He then reacts strongly against Job's unorthodox approach to God. In a speech that almost seems designed to separate Job further from God, Zophar says that Job surely would not talk like that if he understood about God. He is higher than heaven and deeper than Sheol. No one can confront him. Job cannot know anything nor do anything (11:7–10). Faith for Zophar is based on doctrine, primarily the doctrine of retribution, not on personal encounter. God is a highly exalted computer, dispensing justice dispassionately. The perfection and mystery of God does not include emotions or the complexities of personality. Eliphaz used wisdom's theology of divine remoteness to encourage Job. Now Zophar develops this aloofness of

God in an effort to protect his beliefs about God from Job's challenging search.

The author's literary skill as well as his concern to criticize orthodox wisdom is clearly seen in this speech. According to Zophar, if only God would speak he would expound wisdom. But God, who is known in wisdom primarily through observation of the world, is speaking clearly. If only Zophar had ears to hear and eyes to see, he would know that the innocent, suffering Job denies his theology of retribution. But for Zophar doctrinal belief excludes the possibility of investigation. Then adding paradox on top of irony, the author has Zophar speak with authority about the unknowable nature of God. And on his sure knowledge of what this unknowable God demands, he exhorts Job to repent if he wishes to be restored to peace and well-being.

Eliphaz, on the authority of divine revelation through a dream, encouraged Job to have hope because of his innocence. Bildad, on the authority of the elders, consoled Job with the reassurance that if he is innocent then he will again know prosperity. Zophar, expounding on the unknowable perfection of God, prompts Job to repent if he wishes restoration. The earlier implied judgment of the friends has now become an articulate doubt about Job's integrity. And God, who was known through dreams and by the authority of seasoned observation, is now the unapproachable, inscrutable enforcer of retribution.

Job's resentment of his friends' judgment and aloofness is growing. He responds to Zophar with a speech that expresses his growing anger and denounces their disdain (12:1–13:19). Though they look down on him, Job affirms that he is innocent and blameless. Nor does he fall short of them in any way (12:1–5;13:1 ff). Then in a parody of their instruction he insists that he can portray God's might even more effectively than they. Sarcastically he praises the God who withholds water to cause drought and pours it forth to cause floods. Judges are made into fools, the power of kings is broken, and priests are made to behave like idiots. He determines the destinies of nations bringing down great nations to wander blindly (12:7–22). Clearly this is not a hymn of praise like other hymns in the Bible. The majesty of God is portrayed with an emphasis on the negative, destructive character of his power. Having parodied the friends, he then turns and says that he would speak with the Almighty (13:3).

This is the first time in the dialogue that Job has raised the problem of his suffering and the justice of God, and we see that Job too believes the orthodox creed. All his beliefs tell him that it is God who is punishing him (12:7–9). It is, of course, on this basis that he desires to take his case to God. He knows himself innocent. God will vindicate him (13:14–19).

Even beyond Job's belief that God will exonerate him, we see his orthodoxy in relation to the friends. He uses the theology of retribution to warn the friends that their distortion of the truth on God's behalf will not win God's praise.

> Is it on God's behalf that you speak so wickedly,
> or in his defence that you allege what is false?
> Must you take God's part,
> or put his case for him?
> He will most surely expose you
> if you take his part by falsely accusing me.
>
> [13:7 ff, 10]

The concern of the author to defend the downcast shows through in this speech when through Job he says that those who are at ease and prosperous look down with contempt on the unfortunate (12:5). Job is clearly innocent; there is a larger lesson here concerning all the dispossessed. In his next speech, Job makes this point even more clearly.

> If you and I were to change places,
> I could talk like you;
> how I could harangue you
> and wag my head at you!
> But no, I would speak words of encouragement,
> and then my condolences would flow in streams.
>
> [16:4 ff]

In the face of his friends' growing censure, Job makes one last plea that they will stop reproaching him, that they will at least have pity on him (19:2–6, 21 ff). Finally, as the friends continue to preach at him, Job attacks orthodox wisdom (chap. 21). He begins by telling the friends that true ministry would be to quietly listen:

> Listen to me, do but listen,
> and let that be the comfort you offer me.
>
> [21:2]

He then goes on to repudiate everything they have told him.

> Why do the wicked enjoy long life,
> hale in old age, and great and powerful?
> They live to see their children settled,
> their kinsfolk and descendants flourishing;

their families are secure and safe;
the rod of God's justice does not reach them.

. . . .

Their lives close in prosperity,
and they go down to Sheol in peace.
To God they say, "Leave us alone;
we do not want to know your ways.
What is the Almighty that we should worship him,
or what should we gain by seeking his favor?"

[21:7–9, 13–15]

The closing insult to justice is that even in death there is
no moment of truth. The prosperous sinner is given an
elaborate funeral and carried to his grave in pomp and
honor (21:32 ff).

It is a mistake to interpret this speech of Job as the
presentation of an alternative philosophical view. Clearly
Job's philosophical position that the wicked always pros-
per is as indefensible as the friends' position that the
wicked are always punished. Job is not arguing philosophy; he is not presenting evidence of a contrary position;
Job is attacking the friends, since that is what they have
been doing to him. In this chapter we see clearly how
important it is to realize that the Book of Job is a dramatic
story and not a philosophical dialogue. The friends are
discussing philosophy, but Job is on an entirely different
level. His speeches are all expressions of feeling. Chapter
21 is an emotional attack, not a philosophical treatise. The
whole point of the speech is summed up in the last verse:

How futile, then, is the comfort you offer me!
How false your answers ring!

[21:34]

Job has taken a long time to attack his friends. He began with a simple expression of his pain and despair (chap. 3). In the face of his friends' consolation, Job, the believer in orthodox wisdom, considered appealing to God to vindicate him (chaps. 9 and 10). He first raised the question whether his suffering was justified when he parodied the orthodox description (i.e., the friends' description) of God's omnipotence (chap. 12). But it is only after many prayers and the friends' final rejection that Job, the believer, attacks orthodox wisdom.

In spite of this direct attack on orthodox wisdom, Job does not blaspheme God. He has declared himself innocent. He has accused God of causing his troubles. He has now declared that there is no punishment for the wicked. But he has not reached and never does reach the obvious conclusion that God is an unjust tyrant.[2] The closest Job comes to blasphemy is the parody of wisdom in chapter 12. In all of these speeches to the friends, Job is primarily attacking their judgmental attitudes. He is not thinking consistently or theologically. Any blasphemy uttered by Job is by implication and is not stated directly.

Job changes from expressing his pain to defending his integrity and then to attacking orthodoxy. The friends also change their attitudes during the dialogue. Slowly they become more rigid in their philosophy and more and more hostile toward Job. They are concerned with religious dogma and are intent upon maintaining the accepted beliefs. They follow two basic lines of defense.

The first line of defense open to the friends is to prove that Job has sinned. Zophar (the third friend to speak) is the first to directly accuse Job of sinning, "Know then that God exacts from you less than your sin deserves" (11:6). In the second cycle of speeches all three friends, clearly insulted by Job's ungratefulness for their comfort, change their viewpoint. No longer do they say that God will see Job through if he believes. In place of advice, they give vivid descriptions of the fall of the wicked. They are not unlike an evangelist preacher who, having a poor response to his altar call, shouts louder about the wrath of God and the horrors of Hell. Job's attack on orthodox wisdom in chapter 21 is in response to these exhortations. Finally, in chapter 22 Eliphaz goes so far as to accuse Job of great sin and call for him to repent. Rather than change his theology, Eliphaz would twist reality and falsely indict Job.

The second line of defense is to place God and wisdom theology beyond the reach of criticism. In the first cycle the revealing activity of God changes from a personal revelation in a dream (Eliphaz), to the revelation as known by the authority of the elders (Bildad), to Zophar's assertion of reverential agnosticism. God is beyond human thought and orthodox wisdom tells what can be known about him. Eliphaz combines both lines of defense in his second speech when he asserts that Job's refusal to be penitent is sacrilegious and therefore his sin.

Why! you even banish the fear of God from your mind,
usurping the sole right to speak in his presence;
your iniquity dictates what you say,
and deceit is the language of your choice,
You are condemned out of your own mouth, not by me;
your own lips give evidence against you.

[15:4–6]

When Job directly attacks orthodoxy (chap. 21), the friends try to place God beyond Job's reach. Eliphaz, in the same speech in which he falsely accuses Job of sins, begins by saying God is not pleased even if a man's conduct is perfect (22:2 ff). Bildad follows with a similar exaltation of God and deprecation of man:

> Authority and awe rest with him [God]
> who has established peace in his realm on high.
>
> . . . .
>
> If the circling moon is found wanting,
> and the stars are not innocent in his eyes,
> much more so man who is but a maggot,
> mortal man who is only a worm.
>
> [25:2,5 ff]

To preserve the dogma of retribution, the friends postulate a deistic god who cares nothing for man and who is primarily a theological principle.

What began as friendship, but on two different levels, is now deep antagonism and still on two different levels. Job, the sufferer, began with an emotional outpouring of his pain and has concluded with an emotional attack of the friends' theology. The friends, the orthodox churchmen, responded with theological advice and have concluded with dogmatic attack.

Judgment and defense

The dynamic involved in the conflict between Job and his friends is the well known psychological phenomenon of judgment and defensive reaction. This dynamic is one of the most common causes of human conflict. One person judges another, either by implication or by directly criticizing him. The other person who feels judged responds defensively.

The defensive reaction is particularly prevalent in a world that places great value on success and works (as the

wise man's world did and as ours does). We evaluate our
worth on the basis of our success and our accomplish-
ments. If anyone implies in any way that we have not
fulfilled our role or have not done as we ought, we jump to
our own defense immediately and vehemently! The man
who is rebuffed automatically thinks of a thousand good
reasons to excuse himself. If accused of cowardice, every
occasion on which he has shown courage comes to his
mind. If lying be the charge, he immediately considers
how often others lie and judges himself too candid. This
defensive mechanism is universal; aggressiveness or flight
are the immediate responses to criticism. When the
accused responds aggressively, the conflict is full blown.

For example, the Smiths, a typical family, take many
magazines. *The Saturday Review* is Mr. Smith's favorite—a
magazine for quiet, relaxed reading. Unfortunately, Mr.
Smith has little time for such quiet reading, and the stack
of unread *Saturday Reviews* dates back four years. Then
one day he has the chance to glance through a couple of
them and throw them in the trash. Mrs. Smith finds the
magazines in the waste can and exclaims with great
delight, "Well! I see you've finally decided to throw away
the *Saturday Reviews.*"

In a response designed to justify his habits, Mr. Smith
replies, "I was only keeping them until I had a chance to
read them." And then adds his attack, "If I didn't have to
do so much work around here, maybe I would have time
to sit down and read."

"I only wanted to thank you for cleaning up a little, not
start an argument," his wife says as she leaves the room. A
compliment that contained a slight judgment was taken by
Mr. Smith as an attack on his scholastic abilities and on
his intelligence that he would buy a magazine and then not
read it. His very integrity was at stake! But what a foolish

thing to defend; what a shame to attack a loved and loving wife. Yet how frequent is such defensive behavior!

Judgment and defense is perhaps the most common interpersonal conflict known to man. It is the dynamic that envelops Job and his friends. The friends try to help Job. The tragic irony is that all the friends say in a kind way is seen by Job as an attack on his integrity. Job is right in perceiving condemnation in their consolation. In response to their judgment, he defends his innocence. The friends in turn see Job's defense as a personal attack on their faith and advice. From this point the conflict grows. As Job becomes more and more defensive, the friends attack his integrity more directly and attempt to remove his only support—the experience of the caring God. They are caught in a vicious cycle that leads to their ultimate antagonism. Job's final response is to deny that right action is ever rewarded (chaps. 21 and 24) and to place his total faith in his integrity (chaps. 29–31). The friends' final response is to claim that God is unknowable and uncaring (chap. 25) and to accuse Job of sins he never committed (chap. 22). In the beginning the friends were concerned for their suffering companion; in the end they are concerned only with defending their religious beliefs. In the beginning Job sought comfort; in the end he is concerned above all else with his worth.

The fuel upon which this type of conflict feeds is fear and guilt. Where there is no fear or guilt, there is no reaction. If a child tells his father he should quit work so the family could tour the world, the father can patiently explain to the child the necessity of money and therefore of work. But if a child asks his father to help him build with his Tinkertoys just as the father is sitting down in his favorite chair to watch a football game on a Sunday afternoon, then may come an incredible outpouring of excuses. "This is the only chance I have to relax. I work hard all week for you and this family and now I'm doing something for myself. You should learn how to do your Tinkertoys by yourself. Besides this is the most important ball game of the season. If you want to learn about football and can be quiet, I'll let you sit here with me. Otherwise, please don't bother me anymore." Obviously the father feels guilty that he is neglecting his young son and resents the judgment implicit in his son's request. Behind the defensive reaction feelings of guilt are often found.

The success ethic plays its role at this point. If someone fails, the success ethic tells him he is bad or stupid for failing. So said Job's society; so says our own. The conflict in the dialogue comes ultimately from Job's acceptance of the dogmas of orthodox wisdom. He is a part of his society. He believes in retribution. As Eliphaz himself said, Job is innocent. Therefore Job believes that God, who knows this, should indicate his innocence to his friends. After all, God rewards right action. We shall see that Job's final speech and challenge to God is based totally on the belief that he should be rewarded for his righteousness.

Job does believe in retribution at a very deep level. He too sees illness and defeat as punishments for wrongdoing. Because he feels the guilt imposed on him by the friends, he responds quickly in defense of his innocence. He knows he is innocent, yet he feels guilty.

The friends on the other hand react out of fear. Their self-evaluation is also based on success. If Job is innocent, if he is as good as they are, then they are no better than Job or any one else below them on the social ladder. The idea of Job's innocence threatens their total view of reality. Because they have led basically good lives and because they have become successful, the friends believe themselves morally and socially superior to those who have been less successful. If Job is innocent, their superiority is nothing more than a chance of fate. In fear lest their beliefs and their self-importance crumble, they react against Job's claim of moral integrity.

We may think this dynamic does not apply to the twentieth century. After all we do not believe illness is caused as a punishment for sin. We do not believe a man's business would fail because of his immorality. But I wonder. The language we use today may be quite different from the twenty-five-hundred-year-old proverbs which conclude that the result of right action is success and the result of wrong action is failure. But our judgments are the same. All who know failure know the feelings of guilt, even those who are ill.

Although we do not view illness as punishment from God, guilt feelings are present in most sickness. A mother feels she should be up caring for the children. A man feels guilt for the extra burden of work he forces on his business colleagues. Furthermore, the more we know about the psychosomatic character of illness, the more we develop guilty feelings that somehow we choose to be sick. We wonder what we did to catch the disease and how we could have prevented it. Guilt is imposed by a society that values works. We feel guilty because we, like Job, accept society's value system. We feel guilty because we are unable to *do* what we normally would be doing. This is clearly a false guilt. We are not culpable for being sick. But like Job we feel judged on the basis of our situation, not on the basis of who we are.

The same type of judgment and guilt is imposed upon the poor. How often it is said they are poor because they are lazy, no good, immoral, and stupid! The poor recognize that this is an unfair judgment. Yet if a poor man wants to escape poverty, he must work very, very hard. By his very act of working hard, he affirms society's judgment that poverty and laziness go hand in hand. Likewise, if he refuses to work he confirms that judgment. Just as Job was judged simply because of his situation, so to be poor is to be judged by a society that values success. Just as Job struck out against his friends, so it is no surprise that the poor strike out in riots and violence against the society that unfairly judges them.

This same defensive reaction is found among all who are not fulfilling the goals of success. Much of the anger in the women's liberation movement is a result of the attitude that says women are inferior to men. As Job said to the friends that he fell short of them in nothing, even so, the women's movement is telling the world of their equality with men. Or again, when a person retires, he often feels worthless because he is no longer producing goods or services. Since we place so much value on what someone produces, it is not surprising that the retired person feels guilty every day he relaxes. As Job cried to his friends who were using as an instrument of insult and humiliation his God-created situation (19:2–6), so the elderly ask not to be thrown aside because of what happens to created life.

The list of examples is endless. In a society based on success, the unsuccessful and non-productive are judged unworthy because of their situation. We all are a part of such a society. When it judges us, we judge ourselves, feeling guilty over a situation not in our control. This is false guilt. It is as false as the judgment of Job's friends. When Job, out of his guilt and in response to the judgment, cries out, he becomes Everyman. His cry is the cry of all who are ill or poor or female or old or in any way considered unsuccessful. His pain is the pain of millions who have known the false judgment of others.

Job, the alienated man

Alienation is the concept that best describes Job's distress. Alienation is basically an unwanted separation that results in mental anguish. Three factors are necessary to produce a state of alienation. (1) A person must be conscious of a separation. (2) He must feel that to be separated is wrong, and he must desire to be reunited. And (3) he is powerless to change his situation. Clearly if one wants to be separated there is no anguish. If one has control and can change the situation, then the anguish is not great. The whole dynamic of alienation centers on the feeling of being trapped. Alienation is an unwanted separation that appears hopelessly unchangeable.

This concept of alienation is very helpful in understanding teenagers. They know they belong to their families. They recognize the need to be in school, and they want parents to support them both physically and emotionally. Yet at the same time they resent parents' advice, rules, and suggestions because they have decided that they are old enough to make up their own minds. They resent their parents' (often correct) judgment that they are not mature enough to make adult decisions. The result is the feeling of alienation. They want to be part of their families, and yet they feel judged and separated. They are powerless to change the situation; only time will make teenagers into adults.

One symptom of this alienation in teenagers is the erratic shifts in behavior that are so typical. At one minute their parents are the greatest people in the world; the next minute the adolescents yell about how stupid and tyrannical parents are. One moment they desire above all else their parents' love and affection; the next moment they just want their parents to get off their backs. This is the same kind of erratic behavior which appears in Job in relation to his friends.

Of course the dynamic of alienation is not restricted to teenagers. The parents feel the same alienation from the teenagers. One minute the parents want to hug their offspring; the next minute they want to kill them. An estranged married couple seeking to rebuild their life together often finds that they are caught in an alienation-producing trap. They desire reconciliation, but cannot take the demands each is placing on the other. Although they can sit down one minute and truly communicate; five minutes later they may be in an angry argument. In these and other examples the people involved find themselves powerless to change the situation. The anguish and stress sometimes is great enough to destroy a person.

Job, because of what has happened to him, becomes the alienated man. The judgment of his friends separates him from them. At first their judgment is only implied, but later their condemnation is stated clearly: Job is among the outcast-wicked; they are the prosperous-righteous.

But Job cries out that their judgment is wrong: Devotion is due from his friends to one who despairs (6:14). Do not consider him evil because of his pain and his sorrow (6:28–30). He has sense as well as they, he is not inferior to them (12:3, 13:3). If he were in their place, he would not judge; he would console (16:5). Job knows he is not wicked; therefore, he protests against being cast out. His cries of anger show the pain of loss—loss of friendship and loss of position. Job's protesting against the friends' judgment indicates his deep sorrow in the separation that judgment proclaimed.

All that has happened and is happening is out of Job's control. Nothing that he did caused his fall. He cannot through his own efforts make himself whole, prosperous and respected again. And he has no control over his friends' thoughts. They believe what the culture has taught them. The more Job protests his innocence; the more they become sure of his guilt.

Job's speech in chapter 19 expresses the full dynamic of his alienation from his friends. He begins with a plea for his friends to stop falsely accusing him.

> How long will you exhaust me
> and pulverize me with words?
> Time and time again you have insulted me
> and shamelessly done me wrong.
>
> [19:2 ff]

He claims that his sin has not caused his fall. Job is powerless. God has brought this misfortune on him, he cries.

> But if indeed you lord it over me
> and try to justify the reproaches levelled at me,
> I tell you, God himself has put me in the wrong,
> he has drawn the net round me.
> If I cry "Murder!" no one answers;
> if I appeal for help, I get no justice,
> He has walled in my path so that I cannot break away,
> and he has hedged in the road before me.
> He has stripped me of all honor
> and has taken the crown from my head.
> On every side he beats me down and I am gone;
> he has uprooted my hope like a tree.
>
> [19:5–10]

All have abandoned Job—brothers, friends, kinsmen, and even slaves. In a last hope he cries out to his friends:

Pity me, pity me, you that are my friends;
for the hand of God has touched me.
Why do you pursue me as God pursues me?
Have you not had your teeth in me long enough?

[19:21 ff]

Then knowing that his only true hope of vindication is
with God, he turns on his friends, ironically using orthodox dogma against them.

My heart failed me when you said,
"What a train of disaster he has brought on himself!
The root of the trouble lies in him."
Beware of the sword that points at you,
the sword that sweeps away all iniquity;
then you will know that there is a judge.

[19:28 ff]

Job is the totally alienated man. His hope in his friends is
ended. They are destroying him. Since he is too ill to leave
them, the only course of action remaining for Job is a
direct attack. In his next speech (chap. 21) he does turn
and attack them by denying the orthodox creed.

Job's alienation is manifest in his erratic behavior
toward his friends. One minute he cries out for their
affection; the next minute he curses their thick-headed-
ness. He begs them to be consoling, and then rejects their
judgmental consolation.

Another symptom of his alienation is the way he often
talks about himself. He begins by talking about man in
general, when in truth he is not making a point that would
apply to all men but is speaking of his own condition
(3:20–23; 7:1 ff, 9 ff, 17 ff, 9:2–4; 14:1–2, 18–21). After so
reflecting almost absent-mindedly, he suddenly shifts and

says what he means by applying his musings to himself. This may be a poetic technique used to portray Job as Everyman, but his manner of speaking also gives the reader a feeling of Job's alienation. Job is alienated to the point that he emotionally withdraws from his plight. The poet portrays the feeling that somehow Job is above the situation, observing himself in a disinterested manner. This is the same feeling of alienation that is so well portrayed in Camus' *The Stranger*.

Job, however, is in part responsible for his situation. Though unaware of his role and, therefore, powerless to change, he does play a part in his alienation from his friends. In his desire to bridge the gap between himself and his friends, Job cries out for two things: for their friendship and for their respect. On the one hand he begs them not to judge him: he simply wants their friendship (6:14, 28–30; 16:5; 19:21 ff). On the other hand, Job cries out that their judgment is wrong. He wants them to accept him as not guilty; he wants their respect (6:29 ff; 12:3; 13:3; 19:2 ff, 5 ff).

The desire for respect and the resulting defense of his integrity separate Job from their love. The friends would be happy to accept Job as a sinner who repents and confesses his wrong-doing to God (11:13–20; 15:2–16; 22:21–30). Job knowing he has done no wrong, refuses to repent and demands his friends acknowledge his innocence. Had Job been less honest and confessed to being a sinner, even though he did not know what the sins were, his friends would have opened their arms to him. But Job defends his integrity. Though he is correct and honest, that defense separates him from his friends. Ultimately the desire for respect becomes the driving force in Job's life and the basic motive behind his final speech.

Defensive, alienated, and totally alone, Job is the

portrait of a man trapped by the ethic of success. To be unsuccessful is to be judged and cast out. Although Job knows he is as good as the others, the successful view him as inferior. Job cannot change his situation or his culture. He is trapped—as are all people who are poor, or sick, or in any way looked down upon.

Again the author's concern to defend the suffering and the helpless is clear. Job by his very being is the pastor to the outcast. He shares in their suffering and feels their pain. He participates in their tragic hurts and knows fully the sorrow of being shunned. Job also is their protestor. The outcast have no voice that can be heard among the successful pillars of society. Crying out against the world-view that demeans the unsuccessful man, Job speaks for the dispossessed.

Alienation is the product of an ethic based on success and the reality of failure. Job, the alienated man, protests this unfair judgment and warns the successful people that their lifestyle is indeed fragile.

CHAPTER 4

JOB AND GOD

(suggested reading, Job 16–23, and chaps.
24–27 in appendix B)

Am I the monster of the deep, am I the sea-serpent,
that thou settest a watch over me?
When I think that my bed will comfort me,
that sleep will relieve my complaining,
thou dost terrify me with dreams
and affright me with visions.
. . . .
Why hast thou made me thy butt,
and why have I become thy target?
Why dost thou not pardon my offence
and take away my guilt?

[7:12–14, 20c–21b]

Job finds himself alienated from God in much the same
way that he found himself alienated from his friends. Job
comes to see himself as separated from God, against his
wishes, and without any hope of bridging the gap.

Just as Job did not immediately feel torn and crushed in
his relationship with his friends; so in his relationship with
the Almighty, the forces alienating Job and God build

slowly. In the beginning of the dialogue, Job feels only the pain of his disease and the despair of his loss. The dynamics that will alienate him from his friends and from God are only latent. Job first expresses his estrangement from God and his growing sense of alienation in his thinking about death.

Job breaks his seven-day silence by cursing the day of his birth (chap. 3). In his opening lament death attracts Job as an escape from all his troubles, but he never truly contemplates taking his life. Thinking how much easier it would have been had he never been born, even envying the dead who no longer must struggle, Job himself does not give up the will to live. Reflecting the prevailing idea of the Old Testament, Job has no belief in a personal existence after death. All die and all go to Sheol, the shadowy world where one exists, but does nothing. There is no relationship, no joy, and no life in Sheol. Though death is an appealing escape, the extinction of his personality is not. He does not contemplate suicide nor wish he were now dead. In this one speech Job expresses both his affinity for life and his separation from it: the two sides of alienation.

Eliphaz's comfort (chaps. 4 and 5) focuses Job's thoughts on righteousness and on his own personal character evaluation. Having picked up the implied judgment in his friends' advice, Job's desire for death takes on a new dimension: death would not only bring relief from his pain, it also becomes a way of preserving his integrity. Job moves from his fascination with death to actually expressing the desire that God would take his life. He fears that his strength will give out and that, being unable to persevere until God relieves his suffering, he will sin.

> O that I might have my request,
> that God would grant what I hope for:

that he would be pleased to crush me,
to snatch me away with his hand and cut me off!
For that would bring me relief,
and in the face of unsparing anguish I would leap for
        joy,
[for] I have not denied the words of the Holy One.

[6:8–10, including 10c]

Until this point in his life, he has been an innocent man; but in the face of such suffering, fearing he might sin, he would rather die.

Having responded angrily to Eliphaz's consolation (6:14–30), Job again toys with the idea of death (chap. 7). He now considers how quickly death comes to men and how short life truly is. In his first prayer he despairingly turns to God:

Remember, my life is but a breath of wind;
I shall never again see good days.
Thou wilt behold me no more with a seeing eye;
Under thy very eyes I shall disappear.

[7:7 ff]

Eliphaz had ended his counsel to Job with the thought that the righteous live to a ripe old age before they die (5:24–26). Just as Job's desire for death was strengthened in response to Eliphaz's implied judgment; so in reaction to his friend's hope for long life, Job contemplates the shortness of life. This shift in focus from the pain of his life to the shortness of life marks a definite increase in Job's desire to live.

Since life is short, it should at least be comfortable. Rather than meekly accept what comes, Job decides to complain to the one who is making his life miserable.

But I will not hold my peace;
I will speak out in the distress of my mind
and complain in the bitterness of my soul.

[7:11]

Possibly parodying Psalm 8, he pleads with God, the enemy, to leave him alone.

I would rather be choked outright;
I would prefer death to all my sufferings.
I am in despair, I would not go on living;
leave me alone, for my life is but a vapor.
What is man that thou makest much of him,
and turnest thy thoughts towards him,
only to punish him morning by morning
or to test him every hour of the day?
Wilt thou not look away from me for an instant?
Wilt thou not let me be while I swallow my spittle?
If I have sinned, how do I injure thee,
thou watcher of the hearts of men?

[7:15–20*b*]

Then in one of those quick reversals that shows the anguish of his alienation, he says:

Why dost thou not pardon my offence
and take away my guilt?
But now I shall lie down in the grave;
seek me, and I shall not be.

[7:21]

God is too close; he will not look away long enough for Job to swallow his spittle. Then suddenly, Job realizing the one thing he desires is for God to look over him, cries out that God should not punish him, for he will not be here long, and when he is gone, God will miss him. Like a young child who has been punished and threatens to run away or like a teenager who imagines his own death and the sorrow of his parents and friends who have ignored him, so Job in an expression of self-pity and longing for God reflects how sorry God will be when he is gone.

Although Job began thinking about death as a kind of escape from his suffering, since Eliphaz has reminded him that God is the ultimate cause, Job's thoughts of death now become expressions of his feelings toward God. Hurting under what he perceives as God's punishment, Job's response is threefold: "God, leave me alone!" "I must preserve my righteous life." And "God, don't you love me?"

Although these three themes are repeated, death is never again welcomed. In the beginning Job viewed death as a means of ending his suffering and of preserving his integrity; now, however, death is seen as the final, ultimate, and tragic separation of Job and God. There is no communion with God or man in Sheol. Slowly death becomes greatly feared, even by the suffering Job, for death means the end of all hope—hope for a more comfortable life, hope of reconciliation, and hope of vindication. Little by little the yawning jaws of Sheol exert inexorable pressure on Job to find some solution to his despair.

The same three factors that defined Job's alienation from his friends also clarifies his alienation from God. (1) He believes there is a separation. (2) Believing the separation is wrong, he desires to be reunited. And (3) he is powerless to change his situation.

As a result of believing orthodox wisdom, Job clearly sees himself separated from God. Job knew God as his benefactor when all was well. In fact as long as Job was in the top socio-economic level, he envisioned God as loving and righteous. With the destruction of his wealth, the tragic deaths of his children, and his repulsive disease, Job no longer sees God as his supporter. His theology tells him all this has happened because the beneficent and just God he once knew has rejected him. The once warm relationship has been severed, and God is seen by Job as his enemy (3:23; 6:4 ff; 7:12–14, 17–20).

Surely Job preferred his former state over his present fallen state! The desire for health, wealth, prestige, and children would seem to be sufficient reason for Job to want reconciliation with God. Job, however, goes beyond seeing God simply as a provider of the fruits of success. Over and above the good life God might grant him, Job longs to know again the warm relationship he once had with God. Job desires reunion with God for emotional as well as for practical reasons. At first, suffering from pain and sorrow, Job, like a young child being disciplined, wished that God would simply leave him alone (7:16–20). Then in an emotional shift that shows his true feelings, Job laments the lost relationship (7:21, also see 10:8–13 and 14:13–17).

Finally, as was seen in the analysis of Job's relation with his friends, in his relationship with God, Job has no control over his situation. As long as he remains ill and a social outcast, he does not believe that God cares for him. Although Job did nothing to deserve his fall, he cannot force God to vindicate him.

Job's growing alienation is manifest in how he views time. On the one hand, in his torment time drags ever so slowly. "When I lie down, I think,/'When will it be day that I may rise?'/ . . . I do nothing but toss till morning twilight." (7:4) On the other hand, death appears to him to be approaching ever so rapidly. "My days are swifter than a shuttle/and come to an end without hope." (7:6)

Job's ambivalence about the location of God also shows his alienation. God having hedged him in (3:23), is breathing down his neck, and will not look away even long enough for Job to swallow (7:17–19). But when Job turns to confront God, he finds the void, the transcendent God who is hidden and unapproachable.

> He passes by me, and I do not see him;
> he is on his way undiscerned by me;
> if he hurries on, who can bring him back?
> Who will ask him what he does?
>
> [9:11 ff]

Suddenly the God who was too close is too distant. We find in such passages a full and vivid expression of the anguish felt by the distraught Job.

Faith, hope, despair

Job's relationship with God is strongly influenced by the developments in his relationships with his friends. Although Job's own orthodox theology might have led him to see God as his enemy, the orthodox teaching of his friends is the primary motivation behind Job's prayers to God. As the friends become more hostile, Job turns to God in hope of vindication. As the friends' picture of God portrays him as less and less concerned with human affairs, Job attacks the friends and seeks an intermediary to allow him to approach God.

The insight that one's relationships with others affects his relationship with God and vice versa is not new. Many have failed, however, to see this interaction in the Book of Job because they have approached the dialogue as an intellectual discussion. Although the friends are on an intellectual, theological level, Job cries out almost exclusively from a level of feelings. Job, therefore, rarely replies to the friends arguments, but he always responds to them in an emotional way.

The implicit judgment of the orthodox wisdom in Eliphaz's first speech (chaps. 4 and 5) begins the movement in the dialogue. In response to this consolation, Job, angrily rebuking his friend's pat answer, beseeches all three friends to believe him (chap. 6). Eliphaz's advice, furthermore, focuses Job's thoughts on the one they both consider the primary agent of Job's suffering—God. In his first prayer, Job implores God to leave him alone (chap. 7). He desires vindication, but not yet knowing the full extent of his friends' judgment, he turns first to them for support (6:3–6, 14–30).

Bildad seeks to comfort Job with another, more direct exposition of retribution. Refusing to accept Job as innocent, his advice is clear: Don't turn to us, your friends, for vindication. God will restore you, if you are just (chap. 8).

Job does not reply to Bildad's theology, but in the depth of his soul the desire to confront God takes root. In the face of Bildad's rejection, God becomes Job's hope. Job, too, believes that God will reward the righteous. Nevertheless, his first steps toward calling on God to vindicate him are faltering. He begins by wistfully thinking of how impossible it would be for a man to contend with God.

> Indeed this I know for the truth,
> that no man can win his case against God.
> If a man chooses to argue with him,
> God will not answer one question in a thousand.
> [9:2 ff]

Reflecting on how great God is and how small man is, Job takes Bildad's thought and turns it from a penitential petition into a legal complaint. But of course no man could win such a case. God is beyond Job's discernment (9:11 ff). Though he rejects the idea, the thought of approaching God is planted in his mind. Unable to stop his growing hope, he imagines how impossible it would be for him, Job, to confront God even though he is innocent.

> Though I am right, I get no answer,
> though I plead with my accuser for mercy.
> If I summoned him to court and he responded,
> I do not believe that he would listen to my plea—
> for he bears hard upon me for a trifle
> and rains blows on me without cause.
>
> [9:15–17]

No matter what precautions Job might take, no matter how good he has been, God would not hold him innocent (9:13–31). In his wishful thinking about how impossible it would be for any man, even Job, to contend with the Almighty, he speculates on how nice it would be if there were an umpire to stand between him and God. God is exalted; an arbitrator is needed to make God play by the same rules Job must play by.

> He is not a man as I am, that I can answer him
> or that we can confront one another in court.
> If only there were one to arbitrate between us
> and impose his authority on us both,
> so that God might take his rod from my back
> and terror of him might not come on me suddenly.

I would then speak without fear of him;
for I know I am not what I am thought to be.
[9:32–35]

Job sees the impossibility of approaching God as an equal.
But slowly realizing there is no hope of vindication from
his friends, Job decides to take the leap of faith. There is
no arbitrator. There is no easy way to approach God. But
he must present his case, even if it means his death.

I am sickened of life;
I will give free rein to my griefs,
I will speak out in bitterness of soul.
I will say to God, "Do not condemn me,
but tell me the ground of thy complaint against me."
[10:1 ff]

The abandonment of his desire for self-preservation and
the repetitious affirmation of his innocence (throughout
chap. 9) indicate the passion that now animates Job. But
Job does not confront God in this passage. Rather, he is
rehearsing the speech he wants to say to God. Like a
salesman before a meeting with an important client, he
goes over what he has to say, "I will say to God, . . ."
The idea, however, of approaching God with his complaint, based on his belief that God rewards the just, is
firmly planted.

As soon as Job has stated what he would say to God, he
turns to God directly and, shifting his stance, wonders
how he can approach the Almighty.[1] "Hast thou eyes of
flesh/or dost thou see as mortal man sees?" (10:4) Is the
one who looks for guilt in Job approachable like a man
(10:4–7, also see above 9:32)? Job raises the question of

what God is like, and then answers it by reflecting on the one fact he knows about God—he is the creator.

> Thy hands gave me shape and made me;
> and dost thou at once turn and destroy me?
> Remember that thou didst knead me like clay;
> and wouldst thou turn me back into dust?
> Didst thou not pour me out like milk
> and curdle me like cheese,
> clothe me with skin and flesh
> and knit me together with bones and sinews?
> Thou hast given me life and continuing favor,
> and thy providence has watched over my spirit.
>
> [10:8–12]

In one of the most beautiful passages in the Bible about the creator God, dwelling on the painstaking love demonstrated by the artist-progenitor, Job begins to build a theology that will allow him to approach God. The spark of hope seems to be catching fire. God is his father! God is not the sadist people have been telling him. But then Job reflects on what God is doing to him.

> If I am proud as a lion, thou dost hunt me down
> and dost confront me again with marvellous power;
> thou dost renew thy onslaught upon me,
> and with mounting anger against me
> bringest fresh forces to the attack.
>
> . . . .
>
> Is not my life short and fleeting?
> Let me be, that I may be happy for a moment,
> before I depart to a land of gloom,
> a land of deep darkness, never to return.
>
> [10:16 ff, 20 ff]

The total prayer is a full expression of Job's growing alienation from the God who once befriended him. Every teenager's parent has heard this same sequence, an expression of the alienated: "Why are you doing this to me? Don't you love me? Just leave me alone!"

In his attempt to overcome the gap between himself and his friends Job pleaded for two things: their friendship and their respect. Now in his relationship with God in a similar manner, Job, deeply desiring God's love, would petition God to vindicate him. Job's demand for justice and his wish for God's loving care are even more closely bound together than were his pleas to his peers for their friendship and respect. Job, believing his suffering comes from God, views that pain and trauma as indicating God's displeasure with him. Job accepts the belief that God punishes the wicked and rewards the just with material shows of his affection. Job knows he has done nothing bad to earn God's enmity. Whereas Job's friends, not knowing Job's every action, can be excused for impugning his character, God, who does know every action and thought, cannot be excused for appearing to desert Job. God knows Job is innocent. Therefore, if Job could confront God and could force God to acknowledge his innocence, then God would have to reward him with health and prosperity, thereby vindicating Job's character to his friends and indicating God's love for Job. Thus Job's cry for God to acknowledge his integrity is also a cry for God's love.

The two cries, however, are contrary. In *demanding* vindication Job is trying to control God and to earn his affection by good behavior. Love is always a free gift which cannot be controlled! Even a perfect man cannot demand God's love on the basis of the good works he has done.

The friends' continuing judgment results in a growing

emphasis in Job's prayers on the demand that God vindicate him. As they become more rigid and more judgmental, Job not only strikes out at them, but more and more he comes to desire God's vindication. The desire for God's affection is slowly pushed aside by the demand for justice. Since his friends clearly will neither believe nor accept him, God becomes Job's only hope of restoration, and to Job justice appears to be the means to force both friends and God to accept him.

Zophar gladly answers Job's musing concerning the nature of God by stating that Job simply cannot fathom that mystery. God is unknowable, but he knows iniquity. In the first direct accusation against Job, Zophar calls on him to repent (chap. 11). Job seeing all hopes of support from his friends dying, parodies their theology (chap. 12) and berates them because they falsely accuse Job in their defense of God (13:4–13). Job then turns and says,

> But for my part I would speak with the Almighty,
> I am ready to argue with God.
> . . . .
> I will put my neck in the noose
> and take my life in my hands.
> If he would slay me, I should not hesitate;
> I should still argue my cause to his face.
> This at least assures my success,
> that no godless man may appear before him.
>
> [13:3, 14–16]

Job is now the full blown Prometheus, willing to die for the truth, willing to oppose God though it may mean his own life. Yet at the same time he sees the confrontation as his hope. Believing wickedness cannot stand before God just as darkness cannot exist in the presence of light, Job recognizes that to confront God and survive is to be vindicated, for the godless man would be destroyed.

His hope is in the righteousness of God. He has prepared his case.

> Who is there that can argue so forcibly with me
> that he would reduce me straightway to silence and
> death?
>
> [13:19]

In his arrogance Job has asked a rhetorical question; the answer to that question, however, jolts Job back to reality. Beseeching God not to terrify him into silence (13:20 ff), Job prays for God to summon him and to present the charges against him (13:22 ff). But the absent God does not answer. Again hope turns to bitterness, and Job sees God as his enemy.

> Why dost thou hide my face
> and treat me as thy enemy?
> [13:24]

Faith in God's justice led Job to hope for vindication, and hope led Job to desire to challenge God. But the anguish of his suffering and the silence of God dash Job's hope for vindication. His faith torn, he pessimistically considers the future and the end of man.

> If a tree is cut down,
> there is hope that it will sprout again
> and fresh shoots will not fail.
> Though its roots grow old in the earth,
> and its stump is dying in the ground,
> if it scents water it may break into bud

and make new growth like a young plant.
But a man dies, and he disappears;
man comes to his end, and where is he?
As the waters of a lake dwindle,
or as a river shrinks and runs dry,
so mortal man lies down, never to rise

. . . .

If only thou wouldst hide me in Sheol
and conceal me till thy anger turns aside,
if thou wouldst fix a limit for my time there,
and then remember me!
Then I would not lose hope, however long my service,
waiting for my relief to come.
Thou wouldst summon me, and I would answer thee;
thou wouldst long to see the creature thou hast made.

[14:7–12a, 13–15]

In the face of death, in the bitterness of his soul, Job's
hope will not die. Surely the creator God cannot hate his
creation. The pressure put on Job by thoughts of death
leads him to speculate on the possibility of life after
death—a possibility he ultimately rejects.

As water wears away stones,
and a rain-storm scours the soil from the land,
so thou hast wiped out the hope of frail man;
thou dost overpower him finally, and he is gone;
his face is changed, and he is banished from thy sight.

[14:19 ff]

As Job sinks in despondency, Eliphaz unbelievably
responds with the first of the truly condemning speeches
(chap. 15). Job's whole emotional approach to God
frightens the theologically oriented friend who fears that

Job would banish all fear of God (15:4). Eliphaz attacks on two fronts; Job as a man simply cannot know God, and no man can be innocent before God. He follows this with a vivid description of the wicked, strongly implying that one who challenges God is in this class.

The friends are attacking Job's two vulnerable points—his integrity, which is all that is left of his self-evaluation, and his faith in God. Hoping to uphold the dogma of God's justice, they remove God from the realm of personal relationship and project instead their own idea of justice. Their beliefs are no longer tested by reality, but are insulated from examination. Their doctrines about God have become a way for spelling out the mystery of God. In the end the friends negate God because they try to comprehend him. When their theological construct is attacked, they become defensive and try to place their dogma beyond question.

Sorrowful and shaken, Job somehow knows that it is more important to love God, to argue with God, and even to challenge God than to define him. Job is the man of faith because he instinctively turns toward the Almighty in a fullness of relationship that transcends dogmatic belief.

In the face of the friends' continued pounding of their theology of the exalted God of Justice, Job, however, loses sight of the creator God who might love his handiwork. But God, who becomes for Job simply the enemy (16:11–14), is still his only hope for vindication. Job rejects the hope of life after death, but he does not give up the hope, slim as it is, that he will be vindicated after he dies. He longs to have the memory of the injustice done him live on.

> O earth, cover not my blood
> and let my cry for justice find no rest!

> For look! my witness is in heaven;
> there is one on high ready to answer for me.
>
> [16:18 ff]

Affirming that God will be a witness coming to his defense, Job again expresses faith in the God of righteousness, faith that is as strong as his protest against the friends' false judgment. But because the hope of vindication is so slim, despair returns as death exerts its inexorable pressure on Job (chap. 17).

> My mind is distraught, my days are numbered,
> and the grave is waiting for me.
> Wherever I turn, men taunt me,
> and my day is darkened by their sneers.
> Be thou my surety with thyself,
> for who else can pledge himself for me?
> Thou wilt not let those men triumph,
> whose minds thou hast sunk in ignorance;
> if such a man denounces his friends to their ruin,
> his sons' eyes shall grow dim.
>
> [17:1–5]

Despair seems complete. Only the bitterness Job feels toward the friends who have judged him so wrongly motivates Job to continue. In a desperate prayer he implores God not to let them triumph and curses them with their own retribution (17:3–5).

Although Job no longer believes in nor can search for God's love, he still believes in God's justice. Rather than turn immediately to God the enemy, however, Job faces his friends for the last time (19:2–20). Describing once again the torture he is in, he makes his last plea, "Pity me, pity me, you that are my friends" (19:21). Experience has taught him, however, not to look for help there for they, like God, are his enemies (19:22). The next time Job refers to his friends he bitterly attacks all they have been telling him (chap. 21). Job once again turns to the hope of future vindication from the hand of God.

O that my words might be inscribed,
O that they might be engraved in an inscription,
cut with an iron tool and filled with lead
to be a witness in hard rock!
But in my heart I know that my vindicator lives
and that he will rise last to speak in court;
and I shall discern my witness standing at my side
and see my defending counsel, even God himself,
whom I shall see with my own eyes,
I myself and no other.

[19:23–27]

Thanks to Handel and the Book of Common Prayer Burial Office, this is perhaps the best known passage in the Book of Job. A different translation is probably more familiar.

I know that my redeemer liveth,
and that he shall stand at the latter day upon
    the earth:
and though this body be destroyed,
yet shall I see God:
whom I shall see for myself,
and mine eyes shall behold,
and not as a stranger.

[Book of Common Prayer, p. 324]

The two hopes that we have seen developing appear to come together in this one expression of faith. Job has hoped for vindication from God, possibly through some sort of mediator. He has also hoped for and rejected the possibility of life after death when he would see God caring for him. On first reading this passage in English, especially in the older translations, it appears that all these possibilities have been affirmed by Job, that after death he will be raised from the dead and through a mediator be justified before God. Unfortunately the Hebrew is not so clear. The redeemer is probably God himself, as the New English Bible has translated it, and Verse 26 is ambiguous in regard to whether the vindication is coming before or after death. The opening verses concerning the inscription in stone suggest that Job's faith in justice depends not on his resurrection but on his words being preserved, read, and believed. If the Book of Job is semi-autobiographical, this passage may even reflect one of the author's motives in writing the book. Unfortunately, the difficulties of this passage in the Hebrew make any definite conclusions about its meaning almost impossible.

This "redeemer" passage is, however, an important passage in the book. Within the context of the dramatic movement of the story two important conclusions may be drawn. First, however one interprets this passage, Job does gather together his hopes for vindication and does express them in an affirmation of faith. This is the high point for Job's trust in the just God. In his unshakable assurance that there must be justice in the world, Job envisions God rising to his defense. God is not an arbitrator waiting to judge him fairly, not even a witness ready to testify on his behalf, but a redeemer who will fight his cause even at the end of time.

Second, the faith expressed here is the hope for personal vindication. Job's major concern is to maintain his integrity. He does not desire a reconciler and is not asking that his relationship with God be repaired. He is asking that God will show his friends that he, Job, is righteous. The great faith, therefore, expressed in this passage is not submission to God's will, but hope that God will do Job's will.

NB

This may well be the high point for Job's trust in the just God, but it is not the climax of the poem, as one third of the dialogue remains. This is the summit of hope, but the hope leads only to greater despair and alienation. His vision of future justice quickly fades. Job turns in anger to his friends, threatening them with God's judgment because of their cruelty to him (19:28 ff). Zophar's vivid description of the fall of the wicked (chap. 20) then produces Job's attack on orthodox wisdom (chap. 21). The collapse of Job's hope has led to the final rejection of his friends. Eliphaz responds with the false accusation listing Job's sins (chap. 22). The breakdown between Job and the friends is total and irreconcilable.

Concurrently Job finds himself totally alienated from God.

> My thoughts today are resentful,
> for God's hand is heavy upon me in my trouble.
> If only I knew how to find him,
> how to enter his court,
> I would state my case before him
> and set out my arguments in full:
> then I should learn what answer he would give
> and find out what he had to say.
>
> . . . .
>
> But I go forward, he is not there;
> backward, I cannot find him;
> when I turn left, I do not descry him;
> I face right, but I see him not.
>
> [23:2–5, 8 ff]

What began in chapter 3 as a sheer cry of pain has through the dialogue become for Job total alienation, total isolation, and total meaninglessness in life. Job exists in a void. He cannot find God. He is nowhere and there is no logic to his actions (23:8 ff, 13 ff). In total despair Job again affirms his innocence, but it is a plea in darkness to the hidden one (23:10–17).

Job has lost all hope. There is no hope of vindication from the friends; no hope of vindication from God. The great faith expressed in chapter 19 has become total despair. The motive for his final speech (chap. 29–31) is not hope, but bitterness toward his friends.

> I swear by God, who has denied me justice,
> and by the Almighty, who has filled me with bitterness:
> so long as there is any life left in me
> and God's breath is in my nostrils,
> no untrue word shall pass my lips
> and my tongue shall utter no falsehood.
> God forbid that I should allow you to be right;
> till death, I will not abandon my claim to innocence.
> I will maintain the rightness of my cause, I will never
>   give up:
> so long as I live, I will not change.
>
> [27:2–6]

What faith and hope never led Job to do, bitterness does. In bitter despair he confronts God directly, states his case fully, and demands justice from the Almighty (chaps. 29–31, see chap. five of this book). In isolated and bitter self-preservation Job makes his final speech.

Throughout the speeches of Job in the dialogue, there is a pattern of faith, hope, and then despair. In Job's early speeches this pattern was expressed in his longing for God's love, which encouraged him to hope that he might debate with God and thereby improve his situation, which led him, despairing of that hope, to cry out for God to leave him alone. Under the judgment of the friends this pattern changes. In the later speeches Job, seeing the all-powerful God as his enemy, yet believing in God's justice, hopes for vindication (now or after his death), but always the hope ends in despair. Three times his faith in the just God brings him to hope for God to come to his defense (13:20–27; 16:18–22; 19:23–27), and three times the final result is deeper despair (14:18–22; 17:11–16; chap. 23). Job's faith in retribution, his growing hope that reaches its height in chapter 19, and then his total despair (chaps. 21 and 22) together reflect his full development throughout the dialogue.

The egocentric character of Job's faith is the reason it inevitably leads to despair. Faith for Job as revealed in the dialogue is trust that God will vindicate him, that God will do Job's will. Believing orthodox wisdom, Job accepts the premise that God will love and reward the righteous. Job, therefore, knowing his own innocence, expects God to be his friend and vindicator. Job's hope and faith are, in fact, attempts by Job to control God. Faith has ceased to be a means whereby Job seeks to know God's love and to do his will and instead has become a means whereby he seeks to impose his will on God. The self-centered nature of such faith combined with the perverted view of God as a mechanistic Santa Claus inevitably leads to despair.

We should not, however, judge Job harshly for his manipulative kind of faith and hope. Even though Job's desire to be vindicated, to maintain his integrity, is a major factor separating him from his friends and from God,

N.B.

wisdom's theology has taught Job that a man must be pure to approach God. The desire for vindication, for affirmation of his innocence, expresses Job's desire for unity with God even while it leads him to challenge the Almighty.

Belief and life

Out of his pain and sorrow and under the onslaught of his friends' advice, Job cries out for two things. He appeals to God for vindication, for God to relieve his suffering and prove to his friends that he is not evil. Job also cries out against his friends' view of retribution.

These two cries are not articulate in the beginning of the dialogue. Job first toys with the idea of presenting and winning his case with God in the dialogue in chapter 9, but he does not fully present his case and call on God to vindicate him until the appeal in chapter 31, the end of his final speech. Similarly, he does not immediately repudiate the friends' theology. Though he declares his innocence as early as the speech in chapter 6, he does not deny retribution until the direct attack in chapter 21. Job's changing position in the dialogue is summarized as the inevitable movement toward these two pleas: that God vindicate him and that being outcast does not imply wickedness.

These two cries seem so natural, it is hard to realize they are totally contradictory! If Job were to get his wish that God vindicate him, if God by rewarding him were to make clear that Job is not evil, then the friends would be right after all. For if God vindicates Job, orthodox wisdom with its promise of the good life for the righteous and its theology of retribution is affirmed. On the other hand, if Job were successful in proving his friends to be wrong in their understanding of God's action, then Job would have no right to demand vindication from God. The basis for Job's cry for vindication is his righteousness. If retribution is false doctrine, if God does not reward righteousness and punish wickedness, then on what grounds can Job demand a hearing?

Job is divided at the very heart of his being. He is caught between his belief and his situation. Believing God is just, and knowing that he himself is righteous, Job calls on the just God to come to his aid. Yet because of his situation of great pain and suffering, Job knows his own innocence denies that God rewards goodness and punishes wickedness. In the depth of his spirit, he believes in retribution, but his situation tells him the doctrine of retribution is not true.

We do not notice the contrary nature of his cries because we do the same, daily. The poor, saying it is all right to be poor, work desperately hard to be middle class. A woman, saying she likes being a mother and a house-wife, spends all of her time trying to climb the social ladder. I, myself, saying success as defined by others is unimportant, am upset by adverse criticism or implications of failure. We all have those areas in our lives where we say we believe something (e.g. faithfulness and not success is important) because our situation makes that belief clear; yet deep within our very being we cling to just the opposite idea and work hard to be successful achievers.

Defensive, alienated, and torn in the inmost recesses of his spirit, Job is the portrait of a man caught between intellectual belief and real life. Yet in comparison with his friends, Job is the one who is truly healthy. Although outwardly the friends appear healthy, in truth they are fearful of reality and construct an artificial world insulating themselves against feeling the pain of others and thereby preventing themselves from seeing their own ministry. The friends are not to be blamed for accepting the standard religious thought of the day, but when illness and tragedy befall their friend Job, out of their fear of life, they refuse to face facts. When the righteousness of Job's life threatens their beliefs, they respond not with empathetic ministry; instead they become defensive, attacking Job's integrity and placing their beliefs in the realm of dogma, where to question them is sinful.

As do the Pharisees in Jesus' day, the friends use religion to their own advantage. They use religion to sanction the status quo and their own well-off and prestigious position in society. They use religion to separate themselves from others. They use religion to stand above life, to live in self-satisfied unconcern for the downtrodden, and to judge who is worthy to be in their elite group.

Faith, in the minds of the friends, is not trust in God, who created the world and who, therefore, is known through his creation. Faith for the friends is belief in a systematic understanding of reality that removes all risk from life. The friends illustrate the emptiness of belief based on fear. Fearful of the world, they construct their own world which, in turn, they fear will crumble. They do not have the depth of faith necessary to face the unknown or to bear another's sorrow.

Job—sick, sorrowful, shaken, defensive, divided, and alienated—is the man of faith. Unable to insulate himself from pain, he turns to God, instinctively knowing it is better to love, argue with, and even to challenge God than to accept an intellectual definition of God, especially when that definition does not fit experience. Job is determined to have a relationship with God even if it means throwing out the accepted theology of the day.

Although Job, like his friends, also accepts the standard religious thought of the day, he does not twist reality to support his beliefs. Knowing he is an innocent sufferer, Job becomes caught between his beliefs and his life. His beliefs are shaken, but he has the depth of faith to face the fearful and the unknown. Though Job's two cries (against retribution and for vindication) are contrary, both appeals are grounded in the faith that truth brings freedom and new life. Unlike the friends who are fearful of the unknown, Job desires to face the mystery. The cry against retribution is a cry based on a faith that is willing to confront the world in all its complexity, pain, and confusion. The demand for vindication is a desire to confront God in all his mystery and unknowableness. Job is the healthy man of faith because he is able to confront the world in all its complexity and the creator in all his mystery. Job, the challenger, is the man of faith; his friends, the believers, tremble in fear. The last shall be first and the first shall be last.

CHAPTER 5

CONFRONTATION AND CONVICTION

(suggested reading, Job's final speech [chaps. 29–31] and God's answer [38:1–42:9]

The dialogue has ended. The friends have proved false comforters to Job. Viewing Job's pain as a threat to their theology, they have defensively maintained their dogma despite the facts of existence and the despair of their friend. Job on the other hand has moved from pain to despair. Attacked by his friends, he returned their attack. In pain, he now views God as absent or as his enemy. Job is alone. In a desperate attempt to prove himself right and his friends wrong, he makes his final appeal.

Job's speech

The structure of Job's final speech is simple and easy to follow: chapter 29 is a description of the past, before Job's troubles. Chapter 30 contrasts those days with the present situation. And in chapter 31 Job presents his case, challenging God to bring forward any accusation that would deny Job's righteousness.

If I could only go back to the old days,
to the time when God was watching over me.
[29:2]

Job's description of his past gives a picture of the ideal
wise man. There is no better or more sophisticated
description of the wise men's concept of success in the
entire Bible than is found in chapter 29. Health, wealth,
and position are clearly a part of that success, but as this
poem portrays success, the most important part is Job's
good name, the high esteem in which he is held by his
peers.

> *When I went out to the gate of the city*
> *when I took* my seat in the public square,
> young men saw me and kept out of sight;
> old men rose to their feet,
>
> . . . .
>
> the voices of the nobles died away,
> and every man held his tongue.
> [29:7 f, 10] [1]

The city gate in ancient times was the court, the place
where trials were held. The ideal wise man functioned as a
conscience for the court. His prestige and power were used
to defend the orphan, the widow, the crippled, the blind,
the poor, and the stranger. Wisdom literature correctly
emphasized the basic function of law—the responsibility
of the courts to protect the vulnerable.

"But now," begins the second poem (chap. 30), all
respect from the community is gone. If we compare this
chapter with Job's opening lament, we see how Job has
changed. The cry of physical pain has almost disappeared.

Now his problem is the disdain in which he is held by the community. He is laughed to scorn by young men whose fathers he did not consider fit to put with the dogs that kept his flock, Job laments (30:1). Not only is Job aware of society's aversion, but thanks to his friends he views God in a similar light:

> I call for thy help, but thou dost not answer;
> I stand up to plead, but thou sittest aloof;
> Thou hast turned cruelly against me,
> and with thy strong hand thou pursuest me in hatred.
> . . . .
> Yet no beggar held out his hand.
> but was relieved by me in his distress.
>
> [30:20 ff, 24]

No one, not even God, will accept Job as innocent. Even the poorest of the poor have nothing to do with him. Job has gone from the absolute top of the social ladder to the absolute bottom. In this speech Job's major concern is no longer the regaining of his health or his wealth; his major concern is to recapture his esteem in the community.

Job alone knows that he is still the same man who was so highly respected by the community. To clear his name he finally risks presenting his case. Turning to God, Job swears his innocence (chap. 31). The form of his presentation is a trial, a trial by oath, following an "if . . . , then. . . ." construction (e.g., if I have not told the truth, then may God cause my tongue to fall out).

Job's oath of clearance reveals a standard of behavior that is not excelled in the Old or New Testaments. Like Jesus in the Sermon on the Mount, Job recognizes that psychological mood is as important as outward act.

I have come to terms with my eyes,
never to take notice of a girl.

. . . .

If my heart has been enticed by a woman,
or I have lain in wait at my neighbor's door,
may my wife be another man's slave,
and may other men enjoy her.

[31:1, 9–10]

In addition, Job justifies social concern on the basis of the brotherhood of man which in turn results from God's fatherhood.

If I have ever rejected the plea of my slave
or of my slave-girl, when they brought their
complaint to me,
what shall I do if God appears?
What shall I answer if he intervenes?
Did not he who made me in the womb make them?
Did not the same God create us in the belly?

[31:13–15]

He even realizes the danger of hiding one's sins because of shame.

If I ever concealed my misdeeds as men do,
keeping my guilt to myself,
because I feared the gossip of the town
or dreaded the scorn of my fellow-citizens,
so that I kept silent and remained indoors:

[31:33 ff]

Job's oath shows us again the depth and vision of the author, who is not only sensitive to the dynamics of

interpersonal relationships, but is also a moral theologian.
In spite of the high ethical plane of this speech, Job's motive is self-justification. Believing the premise of retribution (31:2–3), Job accepts a moralistic understanding of religion which assumes if one is pious and good then God will reward him with a comfortable and successful life. This moralistic understanding has led Job to maintain his integrity at all costs. If God rewards righteousness, then Job has fulfilled the requirements; God should recognize his integrity. Job uses his achievements as a basis to approach God as an equal.

> Oh that someone would listen to me!
> Behold my case—Let the Almighty answer me!
> If my accuser would write out an indictment
> I would flaunt it on my shoulder
> and wear it like a crown on my head;
> I would plead the whole record of my life to him
> I would approach him like a prince.
>
> [31:35–37, my translation]

Job's speech ends. Moralism has led him to place his ultimate value in his deeds. His honor destroyed, he has defended his integrity to the point of declaring himself equal with God. Yet his motives are mixed. Job believes he can be accepted by God only on the basis of his good works. Within his oath of self-justification is the desire to be loved by God and the faith that God cares enough to respond. His moralistic self-assertion contains the seed of self-surrender and worship.

Conscious of his fundamental righteousness, Job calls upon God to answer him. The movement of the dialogue has ended, Job has made his final defense. The stage is set for the speeches of the Lord.[2]

The Lord answers out of the whirlwind

Who is this whose ignorant words
cloud my design in darkness?
Brace yourself and stand up like a man;
I will ask questions, and you shall answer.
Where were you when I laid the earth's foundations?
Tell me, if you know and understand.
Who settled its dimensions? Surely you should know.
Who stretched his measuring-line over it?
On what do its supporting pillars rest?
Who set its corner-stone in place,
when the morning stars sang together
and all the sons of God shouted aloud?
Who watched over the birth of the sea,
when it burst in flood from the womb?—
When I wrapped it in a blanket of cloud
and cradled it in fog,
When I established its bounds,
fixing its doors and bars in place,
and said, "Thus far shall you come and no farther,
and here your surging waves shall halt."
. . . .
Doubtless you know all this; for you were born already,
so long is the span of your life!

[38:1–11, 21]

At last the Lord, whom Job had so often challenged and invoked, makes his voice heard. And what a strange answer the Lord makes to the suffering Job! The apparent issue is not mentioned; no explanation or excuse is offered for Job's suffering; and no sympathy is extended to the bereaved. God declines to be cross-examined. Instead he questions Job, and with more than a touch of irony he puts Job in his place.

The immediate reaction to God's answer usually is surprise at such an odd response; but after all, is there any reason why God should not be surprising? God does not always live up to man's expectations; once in a while God does astonish his creatures. The judgment of God is simply not the same as the judgment of man. We, the readers, become so drawn into the debate between Job and the friends that we expect God to settle the dispute by siding with one party or the other. The surprising character of God's answer shows that God's thoughts are not going to be like the friends' nor like Job's but will bring a totally new perspective.

Those who view the book of Job as a philosophical discourse on the nature of suffering and the justice of God seek in this discourse a solution to the question of why the innocent Job suffers. God, they maintain, explains Job's suffering in a manner that affirms Job's innocence and also reconciles his suffering with the goodness of God. The most widely accepted interpretation along these lines sees the speeches portraying the mystery, the beauty, and the order in the natural world. There is a purpose in all things, God is understood to say. Although Job cannot comprehend the order and the purpose of every aspect of the world, they still exist. By implication, therefore, Job is told there is order and meaning in the moral sphere, though often incomprehensible to man.

This interpretation is easily accepted because the conclusion is a widely believed explanation of the suffering of the innocent. Much evidence does point toward a moral order in the world, and man's reason is limited. The conclusion then seems self-evident: the limitations of man's reason prevent his seeing the higher purposes involved in the apparent exceptions to the moral structure.

Although this defense of God's righteousness is cogent, such an interpretation of the Lord's speech fits neither the character motivation of Job nor the text of the speech. In the first place, Job firmly believes in the existence of just such a moral order; he does not need convincing. On the premise of that order, he has used his own righteous deeds to approach God and to demand justice. To imply that the order exists but that Job just does not fully understand it is simply a different version of the friends' theology. Such theology seems unlikely to pacify the despairing, agonizing, arrogant Job and seems less likely to bring him to repentance (42:3–6). A philosophical response to Job, who is rebelling against impersonal-theological responses to his suffering, would not heal his alienation or provide motivation for his repentance.

Furthermore, if the author does indeed intend to reconcile Job's suffering with God's goodness, why at this the most crucial point must we interpret his meaning totally by implication? Do the order and beauty of the world really imply a moral order? This is the only place in the book where one must discern the meaning in so indirect a manner. Surely somewhere in the Lord's speeches the author would at least hint that this was his meaning.

But the greatest difficulty with this interpretation is the speeches themselves. The Lord does not focus at all on the orderly purpose of all the parts of the world. To the contrary, the speeches focus on the mysterious character of the universe—the inexplicable creation of all things (38:4–15); the mysteries of land, sea, and sky (38:16–38); and the wonders of wild animals (38:39–39:30; 40:15–

41:34). Nowhere else in the Bible do we find so beautiful and so powerful a description of the wonders of creation and the greatness of the creator. This speech is no rational conclusion to a rational debate. Rather, in an emotional barrage, God focuses Job's heart and mind on the sheer wondrousness that transcends thought, on the *mysterium* at the heart of life. The point made by the description of creation is not the existence of order, not even Job's lack of knowledge, but the point is Job's finite limitations. In this speech the wonders of land, sea, and sky do not portray an orderly pattern but a mystery that transcends purpose. The rain, for example, falls not to produce food, but to green the wilderness where no life is (38:25–27). And the animals are not picked as examples of purposeful wisdom, but are picked as illustrations of strangeness.[3] As a rational argument, there is something lacking in saying to the man who has lost his children, his wealth, his honor, who is covered with boils and sitting on a dung heap, "Look at the hippopotamus." God speaks of the incomprehensible *character* of the world, but God does not speak of an incomprehensible *order* in the world, and, therefore, does not imply an incomprehensible moral order.

The vivid and joyous description of nature underscores the mystery and enigma of the world. The dramatic impact of the speech is clear: creation is a miracle—a work of beauty and of love. Even now the words of the Lord evoke in us feelings of awe. To read or to listen to this speech is to be confronted by the mystery that is the all powerful and yet somehow approachable God.

The form and style of the author in these speeches is brilliantly suited to his meaning. The ironic questioning of Job by God gloriously portrays the transcendent God and man's limitations. "Does your skill teach the hawk to soar?" "Have you visited the storehouse of the snow?"

"Have you comprehended the vast expanse of the world?" Job knows the answer is "no," as do we, the readers. We understand that it is by God's wisdom that the hawk flies, that the snow falls, that the world is understood. But God does not tell us; we tell ourselves. We attribute greatness to God by answering his questions. Just to read through this speech is an act of devotion, for the reader automatically ascribes to God all might, majesty, power, and wisdom. The use of questions and irony evokes the feelings of awe and mystery in a way that direct statements describing God's power and glory would not. God's speech portrays above all else the encounter of man with the Almighty.

Job is humbled in his encounter with God. Yet one feature of God's ironic speech is that personal freedom is allowed. Irony is understood indirectly. The meaning depends not on what is said, but on the assumptions of the hearer. The use of irony makes clear that God is not angry. Irony calls upon the inferences of the hearer, it does not impose the speaker's understanding. Job's freedom is left intact. There is a tolerance in irony, even humor; but it excludes anger. The Lord never indicts Job, never condemns him; he only confronts him. The judgment that is made is made by Job himself. In the presence of God, Job is filled with an awareness of his finite, limited nature.

> What reply can I give thee, I who carry no weight?
> I put my finger to my lips.
> I have spoken once and now will not answer again;
> twice have I spoken, and I will do so no more.
>
> [40:4 ff]

But the Lord wants Job to do more than just admit his creatureliness and be quiet. The Lord hopes that Job will act upon the awareness of who he, Job, is—the creation of God—and turn to his lord in worship. He takes up his discourse again. Still without condemning Job, the ironic presentation of God's holiness and man's dependence continues. In his confrontation with the Other, Job is convicted of trying to be equal with God, of trying to justify himself. God does not make the charge. Job convicts himself.

> I have spoken of great things which I have not
>   understood,
> things too wonderful for me to know.
> I knew of thee then only by report,
> but now I see thee with my own eyes.
> Therefore I *am nothing*;
> I repent in dust and ashes.
>
> [42:3,5 ff]

The meaning of the Hebrew in verse 6 is difficult to translate. The word translated "I am nothing" includes the meaning "to flow or melt away" into nothingness. The word translated "I repent" is not the usual Hebrew word for repent (*šub*) which means to change from one way to another. The word used by Job (*naham*) denotes inner motivation. It means being moved to deep pathos, to suffer great sorrow over one's own behavior.[4] It is predominately used with the Lord, who repents of the evil he has done or would do to his people. It is less often used with men's repentance. We should not understand Job's repentance as implying culpability. In no way should this passage be understood as a mechanistic retraction of what Job has said or done. Rather the whole passage expresses the human reaction to the encounter with the Holy One "I knew of thee then only by report, but now I see thee with my own eyes." All of Job's arrogance was based on his hearsay beliefs about God. But before the Infinite Being in whom we live and move and have our being, we shrink into the infinitely small. Job's egocentricity is annihilated. The purpose of the Lord's words is to establish a personal relationship between Job and his creator. Job bows down in holy worship.

We may wish the author of Job had been more explicit about Job's response. A longer speech might have clarified the problems of interpretation. But the silence of the verbose Job speaks loudly of his awe in the presence of the Holy.

How different is the judgment of God from the judgment of the friends! The friends tried to convict Job of some sin that he had never committed. The Lord says nothing abut Job's innocence. He brings no indictment; nor does he declare Job innocent. Job's guilt or innocence of some sin, petty or great, is simply irrelevant in the confrontation between God and man. The Lord does not condemn as the friends did, but he does come with judgment, and that judgment is his presence, his very being. By expecting vindication from God, Job assumed that his own good works gave him a hold upon God. To justify himself Job came to see God as unjust. In his attempt to defend his integrity, by implication he condemned God (40:8). But as question after question drives home to Job what he has been doing, who he is, and who God is; he judges himself and repents.

An examination of the biblical record reveals that this dynamic is characteristic of God's judgment. The Fourth Gospel, for instance, presents the glorification of Christ and the judgment of the world as having already happened. Christ was glorified and the world judged when Jesus was lifted up on the cross. The crucifixion becomes our judgment when we confront in it what man does to God and what God does for man. The judgment of God is really a self-judgment—a new seeing, discovered when one confronts the Other.

The God of the Bible is a loving God, a God of grace, who strives to bring people to himself, who enters into relationship with them, who makes covenants with human communities. However, the God of the Bible—this loving God—is also a stern God, a God who comes in judgment. Grace is offered to the one who is beaten down by his guilt; judgment is brought against those who consider themselves righteous. Judgment is brought not in order to condemn, but to save, for grace is given to those who humble themselves before God. Grace and judgment are simply two expressions of God's one desire to redeem. Just as Job's desire for vindication expressed both his attempt at self-justification and his longing for God's care; so the speeches of the Lord express not only judgment, but within that judgment, grace.

It is easy to see how God's speeches bring Job down to size; recognizing the love expressed in them is more difficult. First, there is simply the fact of God's appearance—the one thing that Job wanted. The alienated Job saw God as either absent or breathing down the back of his neck. With the appearance of the Lord, both of Job's false perceptions are corrected. God is present with him, and he is not oppressive. Furthermore, while God does not sympathize with Job, neither does he patronize him as though he were an outcast. God does not say, "You little man, you don't know anything. This is the way it is." But he says, "Brace yourself and stand up like a man; I will ask questions, and you shall answer." No one approached like that feels patronized! Finally, God comes as creator. In the dialogue Job's desire for God's love is related to

God as creator. Would God destroy his own creature (10:8–13)? And again, as a dead tree can sprout again, Job cries out for God's love after death (14:7–17). Job's hope for God's care is related to his view of God as creator. God confronts Job with examples of his creative work that reflect the wonder of the creator rather than the rational and useful aspects of creation. The descriptions of the Behemoth and the Leviathan are particularly good.[5] Totally irrelevant to man, they are strange and marvelous, inexplicable and fascinating, august and stupendous. We cannot comprehend why such beasts were created, but one feels that God is fascinated with them too, that he delights in them. He is a creator who makes such strange animals because it is fun to make marvelous things. And he cares about them. The creator is not a super-rational mechanic; he is an artist. "Behold Behemoth, which I made as I made you." (40:15, RSV) The creator, who delights in such irrelevant, irrational creatures, must surely also care for Job.

God expresses love, but offers little sympathy. Job's final words were the oath of self-justification. His desire to maintain his esteem has alienated Job both from God and man. Though in the beginning he desired the sympathy of God and man, by the time of the Lord's appearance, he desires his vindication above all else. Job stands in egocentric arrogance before the Lord. Had the Lord approached Job with sympathy and reassurance, Job would have stood up and demanded vindication. Archibald MacLeish in the play *J. B.* expresses through Nickles what Job's reaction would have been if God had come to him offering sympathy alone.

> Job won't take it! Job won't touch it!
> Job will fling it in God's face

> With half his guts to make it spatter!
> He'd rather suffocate in dung—
> Choke in ordure—

Sympathy was not needed by the one who would approach God like a prince. Before Job could know God's
grace, he must be humbled by God's judgment. God in the
judgment and grace of his being responds to Job at the
level of his deepest need—to know God as creator and see
himself as creature, neither alone nor condemned.

The irony of justification

In the face of the judgment of God, or perhaps better
the judgment brought by Job against himself when he
confronts God, Job repents.

> I knew thee then only by report,
> But now I see thee with my own eyes.
> Therefore I *am nothing;*
> I repent in dust and ashes.
> [42:5 ff]

Job's repentance may be seen on three levels: First, he
repents of the act of claiming equality with God. Second,
he repents of the intellectual framework that led him to
speak of things he did not understand. And third, he
repents of the emotional motivation that led him to seek
vindication above all else. Each of these levels is intimately related to the others; but we will consider them
separately.

Even in his first response Job says he will be silent
(40:4 ff). He abandons his claim that God should act for
him. No longer is Job the prince who would approach

God as an equal to demand justice. Before the face of the vastness of Being, Job recognizes his finitude. The world simply does not exist for the purpose of meeting Job's demand for justice. The creator of the universe cannot be judged by man's standards, and certainly not by the standards of one man!

Beyond this submission to the Almighty, Job also confesses that he has spoken when he did not understand. On the basis of hearsay, Job had made his claim to be equal with God. But now he sees God, he knows the emptiness of his claims (42:3, 5). Job was a believer in the theology of the wise men. He believed that the successful life is the most important thing in the world. Job, the wise man, had brought God and the world down to understandable categories. This is why God confronts Job as he does. God makes it clear to Job that Job does not understand; therefore, his claims are based on ignorance. Job not only repents of a personal claim to be equal with God; he also turns away from philosophical understandings that led him to that claim. In one short act of penance he undercuts a whole tradition of wisdom teaching. Job emerges as the wisest of wise men. Wisdom was not philosophy; it did not attempt to comprehend the world in some vast system of thought. The basic mistake of Eliphaz and company was to overstep the limits of wisdom and universalize an observation that had validity in particular situations. Job now recognizes that man cannot understand and comprehend all of creation and its meaning. But intellectual understanding is not the most important aspect of living. More important than understanding the world is to stand in awe before the mystery of creation. Harry Emerson Fosdick summed up Job's new intellectual position when he said, "I would rather live in a world where my life is surrounded by mystery, than live in a world so small that my mind could comprehend it." Job knows the world cannot be understood in the simplistic terms of retribution. The innocent do suffer. Success is not the ultimate good. The only ultimate is God himself.

On the external level Job turns from claiming that God owes him justice; on the intellectual level Job turns away from the hearsay theology of wisdom that supported his claim. But the heart of Job's repentance is on the emotional level. Throughout the book we have seen the importance of emotional motivation. In the analysis of Job's second response to God, we saw the deep emotional character of Job's few words. In the depth of his being, Job repents of all egocentric desire.

> Therefore I *am nothing,*
> I repent in dust and ashes.
> [42:6]

The desire to preserve his honor had become for Job the single most important force in his life. The longing to be respected again in the community had become the single driving motivation for his final speech. The analysis of the conflict between Job and his friends (chapter three of this book), indicated that one factor separating Job from his friends was his desire to preserve his honor. The friends would have accepted and loved a penitent Job. But Job would be accepted only as just. He wanted to preserve his esteem in the community even more than he wished for the affection of his friends. Job was correct of course. He had not sinned as the friends believed. He was not evil. But being right is irrelevant. (God does not mention Job's guilt or innocence for this very reason—it is irrelevant.) By his vehement denial of sin, Job separated himself from his friends and even condemned God as being unjust.

In Jesus we again find innocence accused of sin. Even in the face of death, he shows no concern that the false charges of the Scribes and Pharisees be refuted. Jesus stood silently as accusation after accusation was presented. By answering nothing, Jesus so amazed his judge that Pilate found no fault with him and even affirmed his innocence.

The sin of defending one's honor is simply the sin of finding ultimate value in actions. Because he was just, Job believed his friends and even God should respect him. Beginning with the teachings of a moralistic religion, he found his value in the fact that he was righteous. When all other values—family, possessions, position in the community—were taken away, Job fell back on the one value that remained to him, his integrity. In the end Job repents of maintaining any value separate from God. In the presence of the Holy Other, Job recognizes that his blameless life is nothing. Hope put on anything other than the Almighty is vain and may lead to disaster. Job discovers that success and justice, which depend on man's works, are not the most important categories in the world, but the loving relationship, which depends on forgiveness and acceptance, is. Job moves from a moralistic belief that found value in human acts to a dynamic faith that finds value in God. Job discovers that his works cannot justify his existence, nor can they give him any hold on God. Only through confrontation and personal relationship with the Almighty does Job's life find meaning.

Job repents of the act of declaring himself equal with God, of the theology that encouraged that act, and of the desire to defend his honor. It is an irony of life that even a perfect man does not have value just because of his actions. Life is short. One's position is precarious. The irony of justfication is that man does not justify his existence even through great works; his value and justification come only from outside himself and ultimately from God. A person finds meaning for his life through the self-authenticating experience of being loved, not because he is good or bad, but being loved simply as he is. Yet there is a greater irony than this. God sends the sun and the rain equally on the just and the unjust (Matt. 5:45). All people are loved equally by God; therefore, all have the same value and worth. The irony of justification is that no one, good or bad, can justify himself; but everyone's existence is justified by grace known through faith.

The indictment of the friends

Job has repented. It may seem that the friends are vindicated and not Job. But the Lord turns to Eliphaz and says, "I am angry with you and your two friends, because you have not spoken correctly about me, as my servant Job has done" (42:7). God does to the friends what he never did to Job. He brings an indictment against them. Another surprise from the Almighty! After all, the friends had been God's defenders; Job had attacked him. Should God not be more supportive of his protectors?

He is not! The friends have not spoken correctly of God. Their god is a vindictive, petty little tyrant who delights in bringing evil on any who stray from the straight and narrow. Their god is a merciless computer that hands out bad times for the sinner and good times for the saint. Their god is distant to the point of being unrelated to the world. Their god is a grotesque kind of Santa Claus, the one who gives you presents if you are nice and not naughty. In no way has Eliphaz been proved right. Job has been right about God, even in his pride; the friends have taught incorrectly. Job has at all times taken God seriously. Not just piously submitting, he has argued with God even at the risk of death. The friends' god was a dead principle; Job's is the living Lord.

In the dialogue the author has used Job's innocence to rescue the sufferer from ostracism. In a culture that judged and cast out the poor, the ill, and the unsuccessful, Job acts as the defender of the suffering and helpless against unjust accusations. Now, in the speeches of the Lord, the author uses Job's innocence to assure us of the grandeur of God. God is not what the friends taught about him: he does not express their ideas of justice, nor does he sanction the rich as righteous. They made God in their own image to serve their god of success. Refusing to answer them in their terms by declaring Job innocent or guilty, God confronts them in his magnitude. Their concept of God is too small. Legalistic concepts of justice do not explain the being of the Almighty. The suffering Job's innocence becomes a means of preserving God's transcendent majesty.

Some believe the indictment of the friends is a bit harsh. Taking everything into consideration, were they really culpable? After all they were only defending the orthodox theology of their day. Their thinking about God had been influenced, even determined, by the teaching of the elders.

If there had been nothing in their experience to challenge their conception of God, then I would agree that we should not blame the friends. But the friends refused to look at the facts of the situation for fear that they would contradict their dogmatic theology. They believed God was just and all-powerful. They were as determined to maintain these propositions about God as Job was to maintain his integrity. In order to support their faith, the friends totally twisted reality. They refused to accept that Job could be innocent while suffering. In fact, Job even warned his friends that God would be unhappy with their false allegations in God's defense (13:4–12 is the key passage, but also see 16:7–9, 17:3–5, 19:28 ff). Eliphaz went so far as to invent a whole list of sins that Job supposedly committed. The friends were not defending the Lord, but the stale propositions of popular theology. In the process they prevented Job from knowing God's love for him.

Furthermore, the motive of the friends' defense was not devotion to God but fear of life. They use religion to protect themselves. Fearful that they are no better than anyone else, afraid that the value of success does not really make them better than others, fearful of seeing the outcast as a brother and of thereby hearing the call to an unending ministry, the friends place all their faith in their self-serving beliefs about God. Denying the reality of Job's innocence, they judge him unworthy, cast him out, and define God as a distant, theoretical construct who sanctions their action. The friends, like many good, religious people, believe their righteous works make them better than others, and they use religion to separate themselves from others. Religion for them is not a means to know God more deeply but becomes a method of preserving isolated self-satisfaction. In truth, God's indictment seems mild.

The indictment of the friends completes the destruction of wisdom's concept of God as the rewarder of righteous individuals. In Job the poet dramatizes faith as complete surrender to God, as complete surrender of the desire to find value aside from God. In the indictment of the friends, the poet makes clear that faith is not belief in a mechanistic understanding of justice and retribution. The friends' moralistic theology of justification by works gives rise to the desire to find value in one's social position and one's acts. Just as the poet saw the need to destroy Job's self-centered concern for his worth; he also saw the need to destroy the friends' teaching that encouraged that concern. The theology that teaches that one earns God's love by good works alienates its believer. Such teaching must be destroyed before one can find the grace necessary for faith in God for the sake of God alone.

Job, the man of faith

Beyond refutation of retribution, the major concern of the book of Job is to describe the nature of true faith—faith not based on reward, faith that would survive testing, faith that finds expression in authentic and selfless devotion. Job emerges as a man of just such faith. What are the factors that led Job to the depth of authentic piety?

First, true faith and the power of grace are found only in embracing reality. We all have the tendency, even the deep-seated desire, to look at the world with blinders on. We cling to our theologies and our ideas about how life is to be lived. Like the friends, we refuse to look at those portions of experience that would contradict our pet beliefs. For example, many who believe in the rightness of the American democratic system have simply refused to look at the illegitimacy of the Vietnam war, corruption in high offices, or the exploitation of the poor. The same is true in theology and faith. If we honestly look at the tragedy in the world, we cannot affirm belief in a god that makes everything come out all right. Faith is not belief in spite of evidence; it is a personal commitment regardless of consequences. In grappling with his pain, his sorrow, his disgrace, and his despair, Job struggled with God the creator and sustainer. In the end Job discovered that no matter what his situation, he worshiped the Almighty simply because God is God. Had Job, like the friends, accepted a comfortable, false theology, in the end he would have been left with only stale propositions and empty doctrine.

The second point the author makes about faith is that to the man of faith God may appear as a stranger or as the enemy, or God may not even seem to be present. True faith is commitment of self to God in selfless devotion. Like Job and his friends, however, everyone seems to desire to use God for his own ends. God becomes the answer to man's spiritual needs, the hope for the hopelessly ill, and the sympathetic counselor for the lonely. True, God is the answer, the hope, and the counselor, but to have faith in God for the purpose of meeting man's needs is not to worship in selfless giving. When a person tries to use God, the Lord in his judgment and grace forces that person to grow until he comes to love God for the sake of the relationship alone. The person may feel God is absent or is his enemy. True faith recognizes that even the doctrine of God as the loving father can be self-serving, sentimental prattle as artificial as the friends' Santa-Claus concept of God. There is a danger in talking about the God of love until one has seen the fullness of God—God the void, God the enemy, God the stranger, God the mystery, and God the holy. True faith confronts God in his fullness and through that experience discovers the awesome God of love, and responds in holy worship.

Finally, faith is not based on a set of beliefs but comes from a personal relationship with God. To enter such a relationship is to be vulnerable. There can be no faith without personal risk. Job commits himself to God, really from the beginning—God the Creator, God the enemy, and God the void. In the faith relationship God gives not security or answers but himself. To enter such a relationship we must respond with our own selves as gifts. Faith is not knowledge about God but communion with God. Knowledge about God may help one come to know God or it may hinder one's relationship. But the goal of knowledge about God is to discover communion with the *mysterium* that is at the heart of the universe. To Job the term "God" was primarily a personal name—someone to talk to in pain, anger, and righteous indignation. To the friends the term "God" represented a theological concept —something to be defended. We have seen several times that Job was on a different level from his friends. The friends were on the level of theological debate; but Job, the man of faith, was on the path toward personal encounter.

CHAPTER 6

A THEOLOGY
OF GRACE

Hard it is, very hard,
To travel up the slow and stony road
To Calvary, to redeem mankind; far better
To make but one resplendent miracle,
Lean through the cloud, lift the right hand
    of power
And with sudden lightning smite the world
    perfect.
Yet this was not God's way, Who had the power,
But set it by,
Choosing the cross, the thorn, the sorrowful
    wounds.
    ["The Choice of the Cross," Dorothy Sayers]

In Jesus of Nazareth, as in Job, we see the innocent man unjustly and cruelly afflicted with shame, sorrow, pain, suffering, and this time death. What is the relationship between these two men of sorrow? How does the revelation of God found in Job's story relate to the revelation of God discovered in the Christ's story? How does Job help me understand my faith in and through Christ Jesus?

Job is trapped. Unable to control his situation or the attitudes of those around him, he searches for some way out of the engulfing web. In his hopes (which he rejects) for a redeemer and for life after death we find him anticipating two important Christian understandings.

In portraying the human situation of division within himself and isolation from society and God, Job represents all men. Job, the portrait of frail man trapped by a judgmental society, is unrelated to the transcendent and omnipotent God. Caught in this situation Job begins to search for a way to confront God. In his separation from God he shows us man's need for the New Testament revelation of God in Christ and he articulates this need for the incarnate Messiah in his hopes (which run through chapter 19) that someone will reconcile him with the transcendent deity.

Job needs the Christ that he may know that God is neither antagonistic nor distant and uninvolved. But Job demanded a vindicator who would allow Job to approach God as an equal, who would allow Job to force God to do Job's will and reward him for his righteousness. God does reconcile Job, not by doing Job's will, but by coming in power and might, humbling Job and annihilating his self-concern.

The picture of the Lord in the Old Testament and the picture of Christ in the New give us a portrait of God who is both a God of love and a God of judgment. Grace is for the sinner and judgment for the self-righteous. Unfortunately, people tend to pick out precisely those passages that are not addressed to them. The man under a burden of guilt sees only the God of judgment; the man who is self-satisfied and contemptuous notices the assurances of grace. The author of Job perceived this characteristic of human nature. Although Job wanted a vindicator, he needed the humbling reconciler. Job found faith not through a mediator who showed him sympathy but through the transcendent deity who brought grace by means of judgment. The situation of Job shows the need of man for a redeemer, but it shows the need for the full Christ—the Christ who came in judgment decrying pharisaical piety as well as the Christ who came in loving concern for the poor, the outcast, and the sinners. The revelation of God in Christ does not give us a hold on God. Through Jesus the Christ we come to know God and in knowing him we come to seek first his kingdom and his will.

Job's thoughts about death also provide an understanding out of which the New Testament belief in life after death emerges. He desires death as an escape from his trouble, he longs for it as a means of preserving his integrity, and at least twice he thinks of the horror of death because God will no longer be looking over his servant Job (7:21; 14:10–17). He wishes for more than Sheol because he longs for God's loving care.[1] This longing for God's care which he had known—the source of Job's desire for life after death—is the basis of the Christian belief in life eternal. Having experienced God's loving care now, we know that not even death can separate us from the love of God in Christ (Rom. 8:31 ff). The belief in life beyond death does not come ultimately from man's need for retribution beyond the grave. We should not believe in life after death because we want the wicked punished and the righteous rewarded. Nor does the belief depend on any doctrine of immortality of the soul or any experience of ghosts. Rather, we believe in eternal life because of our present experience of who God is. We know God now; we know he loves us; and we know that death cannot destroy that love. Eternal life begins in the present experience of the power and love of God. We are made for God. Full peace will be found when we behold him face to face.

Finally, we may see Job as a type, anticipating Christ himself—his purity, his agony, the vision of God, and the deliverance of man. Job is without offense. And though he does not willingly accept it, his suffering acts to redeem man from the judgmental, destructive theology of retribution. Job affirms to all who endure pain that all suffering is not the result of sin and certainly not the result of the sin of the distressed person. Job in his suffering offers to the sufferer the noncondemning comfort that his friends were (and often are) unable to give. The agony of pain and the despair of the absence of God are shared by the verbose sufferer. Job, the Everyman, cries out for the poor, the sick, the old, the female—all the dispossessed—against the unfair judgments of others. Job liberates us from the petty tyrant-god who, like a merciless computer, would reward goodness and punish evil. On the cross, Christ makes it clear once and for all that the innocent do suffer. The mystery of God and of suffering remains. But just as the sufferer discovers in Job a brother who affirms his innocence, so in the cross he encounters a God who suffers with him. The Christian faith affirms that God is involved. But the promise of Christianity is not that faith will bring the believer comfort and security. The promise is that we will share in God's anguish (we will take up our crosses) and that the sharing is all we need/

A prelude to Saint Paul

Job is not only the innocent sufferer; he is also the man of faith. The deepest significance of the book for the Christian is found in what the drama portrays concerning the nature of man's relationship with God. Job proclaims the good news in and of itself—the good news that man relates to God through personal encounter and not on the basis of works. The good news found in Job is a parallel expression of the good news of the New Testament.

The closest relationship between Job and New Testament theology is found not in the gospels but in the writings of Paul, who likewise is deeply concerned with faith and works. The Book of Job provides more than just a background for Pauline theology; it anticipates the impossibility of moralism and opts for faith based on personal encounter with God. Although there is no evidence that Paul's thought derives from Job, the good news of the Book of Job corresponds closely to much of Paul's proclamation.

If one were to attempt to summarize the good news expressed by the drama of Job, he could find no better summary than "justification by grace through faith." The book portrays the perfect man whose change of fortune brings sorrow, pain, and loss of meaning in his life. Knowing himself innocent, but condemned by his friends, Job feels betrayed by God. Accepting the theology of retribution, he believes God should reward his good works with the "good life." He is operating on the basis of the doctrine of justification by works. But Job's works do not give meaning to his life now, nor do they give him any hold on God or his friends. Just the opposite is true. The theology of retribution condemns Job as a sinner, and his own faith in his good works leads to his total isolation, despair, and alienation. There is no better portrayal in the Bible or elsewhere of the "bad news" of justification by works.

Out of his anguish Job finds his true worth in the personal encounter with God. In the confrontation with God, Job bows down in worship, "I am nothing. I repent. Now I see thee with my own eyes." Now no longer concerned primarily with his own worth, Job is drawn from his self-centeredness by the presence of the Holy Other. The pain and sorrow remain. (Even the ending of the folk tale with its rewards cannot replace the lost children or heal the emotional scars.) But in selfless devotion Job's life finds meaning. At one with God and his friends (42:7–9), Job discovers true value for his life in and through the personal relationship of faith. Or in summary, Job finds meaning for his life and is reconciled with God and friends, not by his own good works, but by God's gracious action which Job knows through the relationship of faith.

The book of Job is a dramatization anticipating Paul's theology of justification. Job focuses more on the negative side of justification—we do not have value or relationships just because we are morally good—while Paul, having experienced the revelation of Jesus Christ, is able to focus more closely on the positive—our value and our relationships are based on God's loving acceptance of us as we are. But both Job and Paul express basically the same concept. The different perspectives of the two writers give us deeper insight into the dynamic of faith, and Job's dramatic presentation clarifies some problems in Paul's writings.

Paul's writings, for example, are sometimes interpreted as concerned primarily with sin and guilt. In this interpretation justification by faith is understood primarily as forgiveness of sins. Paul himself causes this confusion by beginning with the universal experience of guilt, and developing the position that no matter what a man does he will always fall short of fulfilling the law. Man can never be righteous enough to earn God's favor. Law, in Paul's thought, hinders more than helps man in his struggle to be righteous. Just because the law defines an act as wrong, man desires to do it, and the guilt brought by law paralyzes man's ability to act. Therefore, since man cannot through his own efforts earn God's love, God in his gracious act of Jesus' crucifixion and resurrection has made clear his love for man. He forgives man's sin and accepts man as though he were righteous. When a person finds faith in God's forgiving love through Christ Jesus, then he is freed from the bondage of sin and law and enters the new life of grace (Rom. 1–8). In this understanding of Paul, justification by faith appears to be necessary only because man is unable to fulfill the law. If only a person could fulfill the law, then he would earn God's favor and not have to depend on God's forgiving grace.

In Job, the dramatization of Paul's theology, we see that the basic issue is not sin and guilt but personal worth and the nature of one's relationships with God and with others. Man's sinfulness and feelings of guilt are one example (albeit a universal and dramatic example) of man's inability to find value through his own efforts. Job presents the issue clearly: Even the perfect man has no relationship with God or friends because of his good works; even the man who fulfills the law must find meaning in his life through the relationship of grace. Job needs deliverance from the bondage of law as deeply as has any man who ever lived. As long as Job remains on the level of demanding his friends' respect and God's vindication on the basis of his righteous life, his despair and isolation grow deeper and deeper. Job clarifies Paul's point. Man's inability to fulfill the law does not create the human condition of bondage and alienation, but trying to find one's own worth in righteous action and trying to earn right relationship with God. Man needs to repent, not of a series of petty sins but of the whole legalistic perspective that encourages his attempts at justification through works.

Man simply cannot produce his own value. Outside of relationships even the perfect man has no worth. A person becomes valuable when he is loved, not just admired. Status always sets a person apart, isolating him, and produces loneliness and estrangement. Only love values the other person as he is, patiently accepting him without keeping score of wrongs or rights. Ultimate value comes only from the experience of God's love which frees man from the moralistic bondage of law.

A related confusion in Paul that Job helps clarify is the importance of good works for those who are free from the bondage of sin and law. Paul recognizes clearly that to be under grace is to be free of the feelings of guilt and of the compulsion to do right that both bind a person and may bring him to see his need for God's grace. But what, then, is the role of law and good works? "What are we to say, then? Shall we persist in sin, so that there may be all the more grace?" (Rom. 6:1) "Are we to sin, because we are not under the law but under grace?" (Rom. 6:15) "Is law identical with sin?" (Rom. 7:1) Paul understands the problem; he knows laws and good works are necessary and important; but he has difficulty expressing the reason why. Paul is opposed to the moralistic use of the law which implies that good works make a person better, give him greater value, earn for him respect in the community, and put him in right relationship with God. But he recognizes the need for moral action. His beginning point of the universal experience of guilt and the role of law in producing sin and guilt feelings blurs the distinction between a moralistic use of the law and the use of law as ethical guide. (In his advice to churches, however, Paul has no hesitation about laying down the law as an ethical guide!)

The dramatic presentation of Job clarifies this point.

29

The law and good works do not hurt Job, but the bondage of the moralistic evaluation of self on the basis of law almost destroys him. Job cannot put himself into right relationship with his friends or with God by means of the law; nor do Job's righteous actions give his life meaning; nonetheless, the poor man who called for help, the orphan without a guardian, and the widow whom he defended in court (29:11–14) know how important Job's good works are. The stranger who found lodging at Job's house knows how important is Job's magnanimity (31:32). The poor who received from Job food and clothing know their lives are more comfortable because of Job's morality (31:16–20). Job's servants who found warmth and understanding in their master know the value of Job's righteousness (31:13–15).

It becomes self-evident that although good works can never earn for man God's love or a friend's love, they are still good in and of themselves, for they produce good. A great painting does not earn the artist the right to have every critic appreciate his work, but it does bring much joy to many people, even enabling some to transcend their pedestrian, everyday life. Giving money to the poor does not necessarily earn the giver the faithful and obedient thanks of the recipient, but it may allow a child who would have suffered the debilitation of malnutrition to grow up strong, healthy, and productive. Those who know that their value lies in God's love are free from guilt and compulsion, but the needs of others bring greater, unending demands for good works.

Job, my brother

One way to grow in response to the story of Job is to look at the characters in the drama to see how we are reflected in them. The friends' indictment, for example, shows us the dangers of authoritarian, dogmatic belief. They know God only on the basis of doctrine. They use their doctrinal beliefs to separate themselves from others and to insulate themselves from a ministry to the outcast. To protect their dogmas from attack, they appeal to authority. They express no first-hand knowledge of God; they know him only by hearsay.

Any appeal to authority is in fact a hearsay appeal. Insulating the writer or preacher from personal risk and comprehending the incomprehensible, the quoting of an authority denies the listener freedom and always places him on the defensive, ready to quote a contrary authority. Scripture is so often used in this manner. Just as the friends quoted wisdom poems to beat Job into submission, so the preacher uses the Bible to force people into belief. The beauty of scripture is not its authority; "proof-texting" destroys the impact of God's Word. Scripture becomes beautiful when we take a book or section of a book in its entirety and use it as an opportunity to see into the soul of the author and by coming to know him come to share his vision of God.

The friends, God's defenders, are my brothers, and we are trapped. The Rt. Rev. William H. Folwell, Bishop of the Diocese of Central Florida (Episcopal), helped me to understand the prison such a defense of God builds for the defender. I relate his story of his experience of the absence of God that came at least in part from trying to explain God.

As a priest, seven or eight years ago, I experienced what is commonly called the dark night of the soul. I had practically no faith in God at all. Oh, I believed God existed, but so what. There was nothing there personally for me. I knew dryness was a part of all Christians' lives; I had experienced it before. But this time it was worse than mere dryness; it went on and on for more than six months. This was the only time I have really seriously questioned my vocation, to the extent of seriously considering leaving the priesthood.

I tried rereading some of my books from seminary, but though they had meant something to me then, they were now deadly dry. I had forsaken all efforts to pray aside from reading the prayers in church services. Finally one day as I shared my pain with my wife, she asked, "What do you tell people to do when they come to you searching for faith? Do you give them a book to read?"

"Sometimes."

She continued, "Do you tell them anything else?"

"Yes, I tell them to ask God for faith, since it is a gift from Him."

"Have you tried that?"

She had me. I had not. So I did. And I prayed something like this: "Lord, I used to know you, and I used to love you; or at least I thought I did. I don't know what's happened, but I'm terribly, terribly tired of this whole thing. I'm tired of having to explain you. I'm tired of having to have all the answers so that when I get through people can believe in you. All I want now is to know you again, and to have faith, and to enjoy you."

In an experience that I cannot explain, I had the most overpowering sense of the presence of God in my life, an overpowering awareness of Christ's presence, of God's reality. And I don't know how God speaks to us, but I heard a message and it was so vivid that to this day I've never forgotten it: "William, I never asked you to defend me or explain me. It was the height of vanity that you thought you could. I only ask you to proclaim me and be obedient."

That very moment I was liberated from the burden of having to get people to believe. My theology is not greatly different, but it has taken on new life. I hope I no longer use it to beat people into submission. There is joy in simply sowing the seed; leaving the harvest up to God.[2]

The implications of this for our evangelism are devastating. The Christian's job is not to force others into belief. The good churchman does not need to defend God or to beat the non-Christian into submission. Job's vision of God makes it clear that God is more than capable of defending himself if he feels that defense is necessary. If a person feels he must defend God, then clearly he is not concerned with the Almighty One who revealed himself to Job. Instead, like the friends, he is defending stale propositions about God, propositions that support his self-image and protect him from the world.

The motive of evangelism is the same as the motive for social action: there is a need. In this case the need is man's lostness without God. In response to the seen need, the Christian's task is to share with the other his own relationship with God, knowing his understandings are not complete and being vulnerable to the other's acceptance or rejection of something very important to him. The Christian's job is not to convince the nonbeliever that he should accept a body of doctrine. The evangelistic task is not to teach knowledge about God, but to show a way for a person to find communion with God. Our job is to plant the seed; God will make it grow.

The friends are my brothers, but Job is also. Job knows and expresses the alienation of modern man. While I look for solutions to my problems, Job reminds me that all problems do not have solutions. Some problems must simply be borne. Job suggests to me that only through the mystery and healing of personal encounter can I bear my problems creatively.

Job also reminds me of the subtleties of the culture in which we live. In the beginning Job desired both God's love and God's vindication. Under the pressure of the success-oriented culture, Job loses the desire for God's love. Slowly God becomes a means for Job's vindication and restoration. How subtly respect is confused with love and how easily the defense of honor comes to dominate Job's life,

And Job teaches me about prayer. Job's prayers and my prayers are not very much alike. I have been taught what I should pray. Even though my theology tells me that prayer is a personal relationship and that I should tell God whatever is on my mind, in the back of my mind is a little voice that says what is proper to pray about and what is improper.

Some might assume that what has been said in this essay about God's not being a means would exclude petition and intercession from prayer. Just the opposite is true. Job has made it clear that the way of true faith is the way of personal encounter. If someone I love is sick, how can there be a personal relationship unless I share my concern. Besides, God in his mystery might just surprise me by healing the one for whom I pray. The point is that we do not control God, no matter how sincerely we believe. Our knowledge about God is imperfect. Job found communion with God because he did not allow his knowledge about God to restrict his prayers (as his friends urged he do). Similarly, if we allow our imperfect knowledge about God to restrict our prayers, we will not discover communion with him.

I am often asked by parents what they should do about their child who is praying for a bicycle. The parents tell me they are not going to give him a bicycle and they are concerned what will happen if he feels his prayer is unanswered. They want to tell him it is wrong to ask God for a bicycle. The implication is that he should pray only for "spiritual" things. Such a solution helps push God out of the child's life. My advice is to allow the child to pray for anything he wishes, God is capable of handling a child's simple prayer.

Above all else I receive from Job, my brother, his vision of the transcendent Lord; a vision that provides a corrective for much Christian theology which tends to stress the immanence of God's love in Christ. As a result of Christ's revelation of God's love to us, we, as Christians, do not view God as distant and immovable as Job did. Written in response to the reconciling act of God in Christ, most of the New Testament and much Christian theology emphasizes the immanence of God. Sometimes we are even tempted to make God our buddy. Job, to the contrary, makes clear that the transcendence of God is as important in reconciling God and man as is the recognition of his immanence. Ultimately, if God is my buddy, is he worshipful? Unless I am caught up in the self-giving act of awe before the Holy, can I truly discover the God-centered character of justification through grace. The full depth of meaning in my life is found only when I encounter and am confronted by God in his fullness—the God of judgment and the God of grace, the immanent God and the transcendent God.

AUTHOR'S POSTSCRIPT

When I become sick, I call a doctor. When I have a personal problem, I sit down with a confidant and try to work it out. If I have monetary problems, I seek help from a banker friend. Almost everything I do, I do without reference to God. My grandfather likewise would have called a doctor, confided in a friend, or talked with a business associate; but he also in each case would have automatically prayed to God about his problem. My great-grandfather probably would have only prayed.

When Dietrich Bonhoeffer wrote that modern man had learned to cope with all problems of major importance without reference to God as a working hypothesis, the western Christian world was shocked. It was a shock of recognition, recognition that the unfamiliar image in the mirror was our own. Today, aside from a few sectarians, committed Christians believe God works through the doctor to bring healing. We pray for healing, but we do not expect God to intervene directly. God is a theoretical construct enabling the doctor to bring health and life. God has ceased to be a working hypothesis for problem solving. We now place our faith in man's knowledge and abilities, albeit enabled and inspired by God.

The process of man's growing control of his life and environment began sometime in the fourteenth century with those movements we now collectively call the Renaissance. The expanding knowledge of the world and the universe gradually pushed God out of everyday life. The inalienable rights of the governed replaced the divine right of the king. The doctor and the psychiatrist have supplanted prayers for the sick. Evolution dispelled even the need for a deistic God, who only got things started anyway. The philosophers have based ethics on reason, not revelation. Government, not God and the weather, now gets the blame for hunger and hard times. Though we face many problems, our commitment is firm—man through science and technology must provide the solutions.

Wisdom expresses this same secularist principle, namely that a person may discover the answers to life's problems for himself through observation and reason. As wisdom understands God, he is working behind the scenes, in and through the created order, to accomplish his purposes. The God who searches for Adam, who makes promises to Abraham, who is angry at the apostasy of Israel, and who reaches out again and again to bring his people home is not to be found in the writings of the wise. In the absence of an omnipresent God to enforce right action, the wise men's ethic focuses on success to provide motivation. Right actions bring success and wrong actions, failure. The guarantor of this success or failure was the hidden God. The concept of the orderly functioning of creation, the experience of God's absence, and the ethic of prudence centered around the goal of success are all intimately related.[1]

The same threefold relationship holds true in our present American culture. Our emphasis on success and works is, in part, a response to the scientific world-view—a view we accept and the technological fruits of which we enjoy—that excludes divine intervention. The world in a narrow scientific view has been created through a process described by the theory of evolution and operates within the closed system of cause and effect. The best anyone can do, says the modern Koheleth, is to try to make as much money as possible, to live comfortably in a nice home, and enjoy what pleasure comes. When trouble comes, the state will take care of monetary problems, the doctors will take care of physical problems, and psychiatrists will take care of emotional problems. Massive hospitals, high-rise banks, and colossal insurance corporations are the twentieth century cathedrals to the gods of physical and emotional well-being.

The church has adapted to this growing absence of God with such skill and dexterity that most believers have not been fully aware of the changes. As Copernicus expanded the universe, the Protestant Reformation brought God down from his more and more distant cosmic heights to the level of personal savior. As science defined the natural laws, biblical criticism became a tool for dismissing the miraculous in the Bible. As technology provided for man's physical comfort, the church became the provider for man's "religious needs."

Today for both fundamentalist and liberal, faith has been relegated to the "spiritual" arena. Faith is a means of relieving guilt. Faith helps people feel happy, keeps families together, and enables all of us to face death. No longer a tool for solving all problems, faith is confined to dealing with emotional problems and death. God has been pushed out of the center of life.

In similar fashion the existence of the church is justified not on the basis that it is God's church and needs no further rationale. Rather the church justifies its existence by being a social agency for the poor and a pastoral care facility for the rest of us. And the secular church evaluates its ministry not on the basis of whether it has been true to the gospel but on the success standard of whether the church's membership and financial resources are growing.

Life in the American, secular view has become a series of problems to be solved. The financial, emotional, physical, and spiritual spheres of life are problems solved by welfare, psychiatry, medicine, and belief. Man's being has been fractured, separated, and compartmentalized; and the function of a person's life has become solving problems or producing goods.

A major concern of the book of Job is this wisdom-secular view of the hidden God. Job is more than an innocent sufferer. He is also a failure in a success-oriented culture and a searcher for the absent God. Through the drama of Job's suffering, his failure, and his search, the author speaks about the essential character of true faith.

The pursuit of happiness, comfort, and success may derive from a world-view in which God is hidden, but at the same time this ethic of success helps drive the already hidden God totally out of man's vision. Job and his friends share the wisdom (and the modern, secular) perspective that sees God as a means. "Do right and God will reward you with success." "Have faith and you will be healed." "Accept Jesus as your savior and you will find peace." Job views God as a means of vindication and restoration. The friends view God as a theoretical construct supporting their theology which sanctions their position in society. The modern, secular Christian, like Job and his friends, has falsified God by thinking him a therapist for human problems and by viewing his church as a therapeutic-welfare institution. He worships the god of human happiness, not the creator of the world. And he attempts to force the Almighty to also bow down at the altar of human welfare. Modern man, like Job, thinks of God in the wrong terms, asks of God the wrong questions, and, finding only a void where he thinks God should be, gets no answers. Because God fails to serve our comfort and well-being, we arrogantly deny his existence.

Job provides the clue to our dilemma. The modern experience of the absence of God results in part because modern man's pragmatic worship of comfortable success has pushed God out from the center of his life. There are legitimate reasons to doubt one's beliefs. And yet to spend one hour a day in prayer and meditation is considered a waste of time by most people, including many churchmen. We have to be busy producing or solving problems or watching television. Until we learn to "waste time" saying our prayers, God will continue to be absent.

Secular man, fractured and compartmentalized, continues to run from banker to broker to doctor to nightclub to priest searching for means to get through another day. People have become means, and things have become ends in themselves. Defining God as a means to happiness man searches in the void to satisfy his "spiritual" needs. Divided in the heart of his being, secular man seeks one solution after another when his whole perspective of problem solving is what has divided him. Like Job, the act of searching for solutions to his problems alienates secular man from others, from God, and from himself. Modern man does not need any more scientific theories to adjust his personality or any more sociological answers to his problems. He needs, like Job, a totally new perspective. He needs to rediscover the dimension of the Holy, to be confronted by the transcendent mystery. For in the act of self-giving worship man again becomes whole; the self-centered needs are transcended; and his essential nature as lover, giver, and worshiper finds fulfillment.

In the dialogue, Job learned the devastation that comes from seeing God as a means. In the voice from the whirlwind, Job discovers that God is not to be approached as a means to anything. God is truly God. He stands above all our problems and yet knows us and cares for us. He answers none of our questions; he is the mystery at the heart of all being. He is the creator, who is concerned with ostriches, crocodiles, and wild oxen. And above all he is the Holy Other before whom man bows down in worship.

God is not to be related to *primarily* as man's problem solver—either as a direct (miraculous) working hypothesis or as a theoretical construct. God is to be worshiped. Only in the encounter with the Holy does man once again become whole. As long as he is concerned primarily with himself and his own problems, a person becomes more divided and more frantic. But when he falls on his knees, saying, "Holy, Holy, Holy Lord, God of power and might," then he finds unity of spirit and peace in his soul. There is an irony in this experience. As long as a person seeks peace and comfort, like Job, all he finds is more and more anxiety and quiet desperation. But in the confrontation with the Almighty, as man gives up any desires he has for himself, then he finds peace. We worship, not to find peace, but because it is meet and right so to do, because having seen God we see that he is worshipful.

For me the one experience that brings all of my relationships together is the Eucharist. I gather with my brothers and sisters around the Lord's table. However one might understand the real presence, the nature of that gathered community is greater than the sum of the individual people. Even at the dullest 7:00 A.M. celebrations, we sing the hymn of the angels, "Holy, Holy, Holy Lord," we share the Bread of Life, and we glimpse that ineffable glory. Then in peace with one another, fed by the Lord of Life, we go out into the world. For me that community gathered in love by Love to break bread together is the taste of the kingdom that enables me to transcend my selfish concerns and to grow in the life for others.

The Book of Job proclaims to the alienated and fractured secular man a vision of God who is truly God—the mysterium, the creator, the transcendent, life of our life, who is in our midst. Such a vision is totally irrelevant if pursued as a solution to our problems. But we, like Job, transcend our problems in the personal communion with God, in worship before his holy presence.

With this in mind, then, I kneel in prayer to the Father. . . . May you be strong to grasp, with all God's people, what is the breadth and length and height and depth of the love of Christ, and to know it, though it is beyond knowledge. So may you attain to fullness of being, the fullness of God himself. [Eph. 3:14, 18 ff]

Problems in the Text of Job

As stated in chapter one of this book, the present form of the Book of Job presents us with many problems. Most of these problems occur in chapters 24–37. Chapters 24–27 are clearly in disorder. According to the received text, Job defends orthodox wisdom, Bildad's speech is only five verses, and Zophar does not speak at all. Chapter 28 is a separate poem on wisdom, unrelated in any way to the dialogue. And lastly, most critics consider the speeches of Elihu (chaps. 32–37) an intrusion, as they interrupt Job's final challenge and God's answer.

In addition to these major difficulties, other incongruities cast doubt on Job's being composed by a single author. The differences between the Job of the prose frame story and the Job of the poetic dialogue that were discussed in chapter two of this book are one example of the lack of cohesion. The disconnected character of the dialogue is another. Although Job and the friends clearly interact in the dialogue, their words do not always reflect this interaction clearly. Instead, each speech, whether by Job or the friends, seems to be a separate speech made in isolation. Many have questioned whether the second speech of the Lord was in the original. In this speech, instead of the many questions found in the first speech, there are two (possibly three) long descriptions of mythological beasts. The questioning form so important in the first speech is almost totally absent. Finally, the language presents many difficulties, and portions of the text are garbled.

Biblical critics have offered a variety of solutions to these problems. Most of the solutions involve the proposition that the text of Job has been changed in its transmission. Thus I with the majority of critics believe the Elihu speeches and chapter 28 are secondary additions to the original text. Others have questioned the originality of the speeches of the Lord, especially the second speech; the dialogue; and the prose frame, especially the ending. One solution to the garbling found in chapters 24–27 proposes that the text was so blasphemous that scribes intentionally changed it in defense of God. Finally, many critics say that the overall lack of polish is not a problem with the text, but is only a modern standard of literature imposed on an ancient work. The incongruities and lack of cohesion were simply no concern to the ancient author or reader.

Aside from the general acceptance of the secondary nature of Elihu's speeches and of chapter 28, no single critical view has attained general acceptance. All of the solutions described above have difficulties with them. First, there are simply no clear objective standards to exclude any portion of the book as secondary except Elihu and chapter 28. Omitting Elihu and chapter 28, the order is logical and forms a consistent story. There are no stylistic or language differences that would indicate any other portion is clearly secondary. None of the ancient translations of the book (including the Job Targum found among the Dead Sea Scrolls) indicate a text that excluded any substantial portion of our present text. (The shorter LXX text reflects a corrupt text throughout and not the deletion of any portion.)

Further, although portions of the text were altered because they were considered too blasphemous (1:5, 11; 2:5, 9), nowhere in the Bible is there an intentional disruption of the text to the extent supposed in chapters 24–28. Even in Koheleth (Ecclesiastes), clearly a scandalous book, the only change is probably the addition of roughly half a dozen verses (e.g., 3:17; 7:18*b;* 8:5, 12–13) within the text and an ending affirming traditional views.

Lastly, the biblical standards of unity and flow are much higher than some of the inconsistencies found in Job. One need only consider the Deuteronomic history (1–2 Samuel and 1–2 Kings), which consists of many documents and writings woven together, to see the overriding Hebraic concern for unity and consistency. To say the lack of cohesion is a result of oversight is an insult to the literary skill and insight of the author of Job.

The solution I propose here has the advantage of simplicity and comprehensiveness. The author of Job simply never completed his work; rather a disciple or student of the writer completed it (probably posthumously). This failure to complete his work explains almost all of the difficulties.

Before detailing this solution, we must first understand the method the author used in writing Job. The long didactic poem is a clearly recognized form of wisdom instruction. Examples are found in Proverbs 1–9; Psalms 1, 37, 49, 73, and 112; and in Ecclesiastes 1:2–11 and 3:1–9. Ecclesiastes 3:2–8 is an example of the use by a writer for his own purposes of a poem which probably existed independently.[1] The author of Job used this form, the didactic poem, as he wrote. Within the dialogue one can separate out didactic poems that could easily stand alone as complete literary forms. These poems were either written by the author or were already in existence and used by the author. These individual compositions are most clearly seen in the speeches of the friends (4:12–21; 5:17–27; 8:8–22; 15:17–35; 18:5–21; 20:4–29, and other less self-evident fragments). A typical speech of one of the friends follows a form of (A) a response to Job, (B) exposition of a point in a long didactic poem, and (C) a closing comment to Job. The use of this form suits the author's purpose in portraying the friends as unsympathetic defenders of orthodoxy. There are independent poems used in Job's speeches also (10:8–14; 12:7–22; 21:7–26). In writing Job, the author wove these independent poems into the dialogue, changing them as needed and adding many portions. This method of writing is one reason the dialogue is not more closely intertwined.

Once we understand this method of writing, the reason for the difficulties in the text of Job becomes self-evident. The author had not finished his work. What he had in final form was the opening lament (chap. 3), the first cycle of the dialogue (chaps. 4–13), Job's final defense (chaps. 29–31, though there is some roughness in chap. 31), and the first divine speech. The remainder of the dialogue, the second speech of the Lord, and the conclusion were in rough draft form. Chapters 24–27 were in a very rough form—in reality, they are the author's notes: a few collected poems and some original portions for the dialogue. A disciple then compiled the book just as it was, adding only the notes in 27:1 and 29:1 to help clarify the confusion at the end of the book. The hymn to wisdom (chap. 28) accidentally got included in the book, probably because it was with the author's notes that now compose chapters 24–27. Out of reverence for his teacher, the disciple did not change the author's words; however, he added his own reactions at the point where the manuscript was broken, a point that seemed the only possible place to interrupt the drama. Thus the Elihu speeches are by a student who revered his teacher, but did not fully understand his teaching.

The unfinished portions do indeed reflect the last portions that would be written. There is no reason to suppose an author should write from beginning to end. A more reasonable assumption is that he would know where he was going before he started. Thus it is very reasonable to assume the author of Job wrote Job's final speech and God's speeches before completing the dialogue.

In the Bible frequently a disciple or student compiled the final edition of a biblical book. And in many cases the redactor added his own thoughts. This method of "authorship" is characteristic of the prophetic books and is a part of the complex history of those books. But more to the point within biblical wisdom, a disciple compiled Ecclesiastes, adding a few notes at the end, and a grandson translated Sirach.

Recognizing this solution to the textual problems in Job, one concludes that there was no "original text" that can be restored. However, understanding how the author worked provides a tool to help straighten out chapters 24–27. My particular solution to that problem is found in Appendix B.

In addition to offering a solution to the problems of chapters 24–27, the assertion that the work is unfinished together with recognition of the method and form used by the author, goes a long way toward explaining the other problems of cohesion.

The present form of the second divine speech is

composed largely of a poem about Behemoth and Leviathan that the author was intending to use (40:15–41:34). Logically, he would have blended it more closely into the questioning style of the first speech, and certainly he would have provided an ending. 40:7–14 shows the beginning of this process of weaving the poem into the speech.

Chapter 28, the hymn on the difficulty of discovering wisdom, is a separate composition but possibly by the same author. The redactor included it because it was with the notes for Job. While in its present form I prefer to omit it from a reading of Job, possibly it was a source for part of the incomplete dialogue. It certainly reflects ideas which are compatible with the author's thought. Man through his technological abilities is unable to discover wisdom. Man can do marvelous things to mine the wealth of the world, but all of that wealth cannot buy wisdom. The wealth of the earth and man's technological abilities are worthless in comparison to the value of wisdom. God alone knows wisdom; he created it when he created the world. Man cannot know wisdom through his works; he knows it only through "the fear of the Lord," that is only through submission to God and his will. (The poem is skeptical or religious depending on whether one considers verse 28 secondary.)

A Reconstruction of Chapters 24-27

The fullest understanding of the book of Job is gained only when one reads the entire dialogue, including chapters 24–27; however, to do so requires some form of reconstruction of this garbled passage. The author's method of writing provides a tool for reconstruction. The first step is to sift out the original sources and notes that the compiler used when he composed the book. Then for the purpose of reading Job, one may do the compiler's job over again. The original compiler simply took the author's notes for this unfinished portion as he found them. Without changing their order he included them in the book. In doing the compiler's job again, one attempts to reason which sources were intended by the author for which speakers. While the task of separating the notes has a degree of objectivity, the recompilation on the basis of the author's intent must remain subjective. Little dialogue was written that would "flesh out" these poems. The dialogue will remain unfinished, but this method of restoration is less subjective than the usual picking and choosing.[1]

There are four independent didactic poems, and several extraneous verses that reflect the author's notes and the

beginnings of his weaving the poems into the dialogue.
The poems are:

24:1–12, an unorthodox teaching that contrasts the wicked
wealthy and the wretched poor, concluding that God
does nothing to rectify this unjust situation. (It is
possible that 2–11 might originally have been the
beginning of an orthodox poem, but the author
replaced the orthodox ending with 12c.)

24:13–24, a typical orthodox poem describing the fate of
the wicked. Verses 13–18 describing the wicked men
of darkness (the tristichs used here are unusual in Job)
are followed by a description of their fate (19–24). The
difficulty in number (13–17 is plural, 18–23a is singular, and 23b and 24 is plural) is best understood as the
incomplete work of the author. 13–17 and 18–24 were
originally independent fragments that he was combin-
ing to make a complete poem. In the following
translation, I follow the New English Bible and others
by rendering portions of 18–23a in the plural.

26:5–14, 25:2–6, an orthodox poem on the impossibility of
man to appear righteous before God. I prefer placing
25:2–6 after 26:5–14 as it makes a smoother poem.
Besides, one dislocation is as easy to explain as the
other. We now have a poem that follows smoothly
from the descriptions of God's power over the underworld, over creation, and in heaven to the insignifi-
cance of man.

27:8–23 (omitting v. 12), another orthodox poem describing the destruction of the wicked. 8–13 are introduc-
tory while 14–23 describe God's action. Since this was
originally an independent poem the second person
plural in verse 11 is natural and should not lead one to
attribute these verses necessarily to Job.

There are two speeches written by the author that were to form part of the longer speeches of Job:

26:2–4 is a satirical, bitter complaint against the friends. The use by Job of the second person singular in reference to the friends is elsewhere found only in 12:7 ff; 16:3; and 21:3*b*. (12:7 ff is suspect as secondary, though the singular and the use of Yahweh in v. 9 is easily explained as reflecting the independent composition used here by the author.) Attributing these verses to one of the friends makes interpretation difficult. A possible alternative arrangement would be that vv. 2 and 3 are the beginning of a (hypothetical) satirical prayer and v. 4 is the beginning of Bildad's speech.

27:2–7 is an oath declaring Job's innocence, followed by a curse on his enemies. The orthodoxy of the curse is explained as a stereotype curse uttered in anger—another reflection that Job is in the depth of his soul orthodox. A similar use of orthodox wisdom against the friends is found in 19:28 ff.

Other verses that must be accounted for are:

24:25 and 27:12, which were intended to end a speech. 27:12 is in its present location because the compiler associated it with 27:11 which is also second person plural.

25:1 and 26:1 are probably from the author's notes, while 27:1 and 29:1 are clarifying verses added by the compiler.

This separation and clarification of the notes the compiler used to write chapters 24–27 is the closest we can come to an "original text." The following re-compilation of this material is solely for the sake of ease in reading these passages. The translation is the New English Bible; italicized portions indicate my revision of that translation.

JOB   Chapters 24–27 rearranged and revised

(Job's reply to Eliphaz ends at 23:17)

Then Bildad the Shuhite answered: 25:1

In the underworld the *dead* writhe in fear,   26:5
   All that live in the waters under the earth are struck
      with terror.
Sheol is laid bare,   6
   and Abaddon *naked* before him.
God spreads the canopy of the sky over chaos,   7
   and suspends earth in the void.
He keeps the waters penned in dense cloud-masses,   8
   and the clouds do not burst open under their weight.
He covers the face of the full moon,   9
   unrolling his clouds across it.
He has fixed the horizon on the surface of the
      waters   10
   at the farthest limit of light and darkness.
The pillars of heaven quake   11
   and are *astonished* at his rebuke.
With his strong arm he *stilled* the sea-monster,   12
   and struck down Rahab by his *cunning*.
At his breath the skies are clear,   13
   and his hand breaks the primeval sea-serpent.

These are but the fringe of his power;   14
   and how faint the whisper that we hear of him!
Authority and awe rest with him   25:2
   who has established peace in his realm on high.
His squadrons are without number;   3
   upon whom does his light not shine?

How then can a man be justified in God's sight,   4
    or one born of woman be innocent?
If the circling moon is found wanting,   5
    and the stars are not innocent in his eyes,
much more so man who is but a maggot,   6
    mortal man who is only a worm.

Then Job answered: 26:1

To one so weak, what a help you are!
    for the powerless, what a deliverer!   2
What counsel you offer to a man at his wits end,
    never at a loss with a helpful suggestion.   3
Who has prompted you to say such things,
    and whose spirit is expressed in your speech?   4
Why are times of judgment not kept by the
    Almighty;   24:1
    And why do those who know him never see the
    days of retribution?

Wicked men move boundary-stones   2
    and *seize* the flocks and *graze them.*
They drive off the orphan's ass   3
    and lead away the widow's ox with a rope.
They snatch the fatherless infant from the
    breast,[a]   9
    and take the poor man's child in pledge.
They jostle the poor out of the way;   4
    the destitute huddle together, hiding from them.

Behold, like wild-asses in the wilderness   5
    the poor go out to their work,
Though searching the desert for prey,
    there is no food for the children.

[a] verse 9 rearranged with NEB

In the field they reap what is not theirs,[b]   6
   and filch the late grapes from the rich man's
      vineyard.
Naked and bare they pass the night;   7
   in the cold they have nothing to cover them.
They are drenched by rain-storms from the hills   8
   and hug the rock, their only shelter.

Naked and bare they go about their work: 10
   and hungry they carry the sheaves;
They press the oil in the shade where two walls
      meet,   11
   they tread the winepress, but themselves go thirsty.

From out of the city, they groan like dying men,   12
   and like wounded men they cry out *for help;*
But God pays no heed to their prayer.

If this is not so, who will prove me wrong   24:25
   and make nonsense of my argument?
Behold, all of you have seen these things,   27:12
   why then do you talk such empty nonsense?

I swear by God, who has denied me justice   27:2
   and by the Almighty, who has filled me with
      bitterness:
So long as there is any life left in me   3
   and God's breath is in my nostrils,
no untrue word shall pass my lips   4
   and my tongue shall utter no falsehood.
God forbid that I should *say that you are right;*   5
   till death, I will not abandon my *integrity.*
I will maintain *my innocence,* I will never give up;   6
   so long as I live, *my conscience will be clear.*
May my enemy meet the fate of the wicked,   7
   and my antagonist the doom of the wrongdoer!

[b] verse 6 returned to its place in the Hebrew text

(Then Zophar the Naamathite answered:)

Some there are who rebel against the light of day,   24:13
   who know nothing of its ways
   and do not linger in the paths of light:
The murderer rises before daylight   14
   to kill some miserable wretch:
   he is like a thief in the night,[a]
The seducer watches eagerly for twilight   15
   thinking, "No eye will catch sight of me,"
   as he puts a disguise on his face.[a]
In the dark *robbers break* into houses   16
   which they marked for themselves in the day;
   they too are strangers to the daylight.
One and all, *dark night is light to them;*   17
   In the terrors of night they are at home.
Such men are scum on the surface of the water;   18
   their fields have a bad name throughout the land,
   and no labourer will go near their vineyards.

As drought and heat make away with snow,   19
   so the waters of Sheol make away with the sinner.
The square of his hometown forgets him,   20
   His name is remembered no more;
   Iniquity is snapped like a stick.[a]
He *wronged* the barren, childless woman   21
   and *was* no help to the widow.
God in his strength *lures* the mighty to *destruction.* 22
   they may rise, but they *are not secure* in life.
He lulls them into security and confidence;   23
   but his eyes are fixed on their ways.
For a moment they *are exalted*   24
   but are soon gone.
They are laid low and wilt like a mallow-flower;
   they droop like an ear of corn on the stalk

[a] 14*c*, 15*c*, and 20*c* restored as in the Hebrew text.

What hope has a godless man, when he is cut off,   27:8
  when God *requires* his life
Will God listen to his cry,   9
  when trouble overtakes him?
Will he trust himself to the Almighty   10
  and call upon God at all times?

I will teach you what is in God's power,   11
  I will not conceal the purpose of the Almighty,
This is the lot prescribed by God for the wicked,   13
  and the ruthless man's reward from the Almighty.
He may have many sons, but they will fall by
   the sword,   14
  and his offspring will go hungry;
The survivors will be brought to the grave by
   pestilence,   15
  and no widows will weep for them.
He may heap up silver like dirt   16
  and *clothes like clay.*
Let him! The righteous will wear them,   17
  and his silver will be shared among the innocent.

The house he builds is flimsy as a bird's nest   18
  or a *hut* put up by a watchman.
He may lie down rich one day, but never again;   19
  he opens his eyes and all is gone.
Disaster overtakes him like a flood,   20
  and a storm snatches him away in the night;
The east wind lifts him up and he is gone;   21
  it whirls him far from home.
God hurls at him mercilessly   22
  He flees headlong from His might.
Men derisively clap their hands at him,   23
  and hiss at him wherever he may be.

Wisdom: The New Theology, 1000 B.C.

The concerns and issues of the Book of Job have a six hundred year history that began with the founding of the monarchy in Israel (ca. 1020 B.C.) and the entrance of the wise men into Hebrew life. A look at wisdom when it first enters Hebrew life helps clarify its basic approach to reality.

We tend to think of biblical times as unchanging. But the roughly fifteen hundred years of history recorded in the Bible was a period of constant, even radical change. There were changes in the system of government from patriarchs to judges, from monarchy to vassalage. There were changes in lifestyle from nomadic to agrarian to urban. There were constant changes in alliances, there were exiles and exoduses, times of national expansion and of retrenchment, periods of independence and of subjection. There were also changes in the religion of Israel: from the worship of family gods to worship at the high places, to centralized worship in the Temple, and finally to the study of the law in the synagogue. With each of these changes came a growing, new understanding of who God is and what he requires of his people.

When Saul became the first king in Israel, he inaugurated a new form of government that would ultimately effect every aspect of the culture and religion of the Hebrew nation. There are two biblical narratives that reflect the change in world-view that occurred with the establishing of the king's court: 1 Samuel 13–14 and the "court history" found in 2 Samuel 9–20 and 1 Kings 1–2.[1]

The first account (1 Sam. 13–14) tells stories of Saul's battles with the Philistines. In these narratives all events are encompassed by ritualistic acts or sacred ordinances. In one story Saul was fearful that unless he began the battle soon he would lose it. Tradition dictated, however, that Samuel make a burnt offering to the Lord before battle. Samuel was late arriving on the scene; so Saul performed the sacrifice before Samuel arrived. As a result of this "sin," Saul was punished by having another's dynasty rule over Israel (1 Sam. 13:8–14). In another story, Jonathan obtained a sign from the Lord to engage in fighting the force holding the pass at Michmash. As soon as he attacked, a divinely induced panic seized the entire Philistine army, and they fled before the poorly armed Israelites (1 Sam. 14:1–15). The decision to attack or not was made on the basis of chance. The Ephod was apparently a priestly garment containing the oracle which would respond in one of three ways: Urim meaning one thing, Thummim meaning the other, or no response indicating God would not answer (1 Sam. 14:3,18 LXX, 36–42). Jonathan's tasting of honey contradicted a vow his father Saul had made that during the first day's battle no man should eat. The result was a refusal of the Ephod to answer. Only the cries of the people saved Jonathan's life (1 Sam. 14:24–36). Why battles are won, why Jonathan should die, why Saul's dynasty would not rule Israel, are here all traced back to the fall of a lot, the eating of honey, and the wrong person making the right sacrifice.

The second narrative (2 Sam. 9–20, 1 Kings 1–2), commonly called the court history or the succession narrative, reflects a totally different world-view. This story of David's reign and the succession of Solomon takes place in the world of power, intrigue, assassination, sex, rebellion, and politics. This narrative contains all sorts of events that movie makers enjoy—David's affair with Bathsheba, his murder of Uriah, her husband, Absalom's rebellion, the revolt of the Northern kingdom, David's consolidation of power, and finally Solomon's ascension to the throne. The events are not related to ritualistic acts, but are determined by a chain of causality. Through the operation of natural laws, Solomon becomes king over all of Israel and the Davidic dynasty is established. However, the court history is not purely secular. Carefully and subtly the narrator points out the guiding hand of the Lord. It is God's will, he is telling us, that Solomon be king.

The court history is similar to our own secular view in which events are determined by cause and effect. But in the former view, as we saw in 1 Samuel, events were determined by an active, capricious, omnipresent God who was approached through religious rites and ordinances. The naturalistic understanding of the causes of events is certainly an advance in learning, but the God who was so clearly present in the old view is dimly seen in the new.

The establishment of the king's court changed everything. With the monarchy came all the institutions and officials that were found in every ancient near-eastern court: an official priesthood and temple, scribes, cult prophets, military leaders, court guards, and advisors to the king (2 Sam. 8:15–18; 20:23–26, and 1 Kings 4:1–19).

Many of these officials were non-Israelites. No previous
monarchy meant there were no trained officials. They had
to be imported. The monarchy brought a new cosmopolitan openness into the life of Israel. Learning flourished,
there was an expansion in world-view, building developed,
and the arts thrived. But these developments also opened
Israel to religious syncretism—a threat to the purity of
Israel's faith and a central concern of the prophets.

The wise men enter Israel's life with the founding of the
monarchy, bringing with them a new viewpoint. The court
history reflects this view of the wise men. They observe the
operation of cause and effect in the world. The wise men
are the "new theologians" of the tenth century B.C. They
no longer see God working arbitrarily through sacred
oracles; they see him working in and through natural
human events.

The political and social changes result in different
perceptions of God. The omnipresent deity of the Ephod is
slowly replaced by the reasoning advisors to the king.
Israel begins to experience the absence of God.

Two important figures illustrate the change. Samuel, the
seer, heard God speak audibly. God revealed his will
directly to Samuel, who actively involved himself in
changing the established order. His pronouncements all
came true (1 Sam. 3:7–12, 15–16). Fifty years later
Solomon, the king and builder of the Temple, was known
as the greatest wise man and was honored for his worldly
success. As a writer of proverbs and a lecturer on trees and
animals, Solomon was the first truly cultured man in
Israel. His principal wife was an Egyptian princess, and he
apparently modeled his court on that of the pharaoh
where the wise men held important positions. Traditionally Solomon is the father of wisdom in Israel. Solomon
worshiped in the Temple, but God spoke to him in dreams

and through reason (1 Kings 3–4). The God who was so readily available to Samuel is approached only indirectly by Solomon. The divine voice has been replaced by dreams and inspiration.

There is a radical difference between the pre-monarchical world-view and the wise man's understanding. The old way saw the world as chaotic. Decisions were not made on the basis of reason or experience. Decisions were made in accord with the revealed will of God, revealed through the law or by means of the fall of the lot (Urim and Thummim). Man had basically no control over his life. To the modern man that perspective would be terrifying. To ancient man it meant that God (and the gods) was omnipresent. He had to be approached, consulted, and satisfied for every act or decision.

In the world-view of the wise men, however, man has a great deal of control over his life. From the experience of the ages it is possible to discern the order present in the world. On the basis of that order, the wise man makes decisions. Chance does not play a part. His decision is made on the basis of experience, not chance. The wise men's genius was to recognize that the divinely ordained structure gave man freedom to choose. Man was freed from the capricious God of the lot. But the God of the wise men is far away. He created the world and established order through wisdom. Man does not ask God directly what he should do, but studies the created order and makes his choices for his life. The faith of the wise men is cold and rational.

In Job we find wisdom tested. The secular problem solving and the hidden God are of no help to the devastated Job. But Job cannot return to the age of Samuel. The author uses Job's search for divine support to examine a major concern of wisdom—the absence of God.

BIBLIOGRAPHY

Those books and articles designated with an asterisk (*) were found by the author to be particularly helpful to him.

Books

Anderson, Hugh. "The Book of Job." *The Interpreters One-Volume Commentary on the Bible.* Nashville: Abingdon, 1971.

Brueggemann, Walter. *In Man We Trust.* Atlanta: John Knox Press, 1972.

Buttenwieser, M. *The Book of Job.* New York: The Macmillan Co., 1922.

Carstensen, R. N. *Job: Defense of Honor.* Nashville: Abingdon Press, 1963.

Danielou, J. *Holy Pagans of the Old Testament.* New York: Longmans Green, 1957.

Driver, S. R. and Gray, G. B. *A Critical and Exegetical Commentary on the Book of Job.* International Critical Commentary. 2 vols. New York: Charles Scribner's Sons, 1921.

Driver, S. R. *An Introduction to the Literature of the Old Testament.* New York: World Publishing Company, 1956.

Eissfeldt, O. *The Old Testament, An Introduction.* Translated by P. R. Ackroyd. New York: Harper and Row, 1965.

Freehof, S. B. *Book of Job.* The Jewish Commentary for Bible Readers. New York: Union of American Hebrew Congregations, 1958.

Good, E. M. *Irony in the Old Testament*. Philadelphia: Westminster Press, 1965.

* Goodwin, Charles. *What Is the Point of the Book of Job?* Theological Forum XII. Youse: University, 1974.

* Gordis, Robert. *The Book of God and Man*. Chicago: University of Chicago Press, 1965.

Irwin, W. A. "Job." *Peake's Commentary on the Bible*. Edited by Matthew Black and H. H. Rowley. New York: Thomas Nelson and Sons, Ltd., 1963.

James, Fleming. *Personalities of the Old Testament*. New York: Charles Scribner's Sons, 1939.

Jastrow, Morris. *The Book of Job*. Philadelphia: J. B. Lippincott Co., 1920.

Jones, Edgar. *The Triumph of Job*. London: SCM Press, Ltd., 1966.

Jung, C. G. *Answer to Job*. Translated by R. F. C. Hull. Cleveland: World Publishing Company, 1960.

Kent, H. Harold. *Job, Our Contemporary*. Grand Rapids: William B. Eerdmans Company, 1967.

Kissane, E. J. *The Book of Job*. Dublin: Browne and Nolan Limited, 1939.

Kraeling, E. G. *The Book of the Ways of God*. New York: Charles Scribner's Sons, 1938.

MacLeish, Archibald. *J. B.* Cambridge: The Riverside Press, 1956.

* Otto, Rudolf. *The Idea of the Holy*. Translated by J. W. Harvey, London: Oxford University Press, 1923.

Paterson, J. *The Wisdom of Israel: Job and Proverbs*. (Bible Guides, No. 11, edited by W. Barclay and F. F. Bruce). New York: Abingdon Press, 1961.

Pfeiffer, Robert H. *Introduction to the Old Testament*. London: Adam and Charles Black, 1948.

Pope, Marvin H. "Book of Job." *Interpreter's Dictionary of the Bible*. New York: Abingdon Press, 1962.

Pope, Marvin. *Job*. Anchor Bible. New York: Doubleday and Company, Inc., 1965.

Robinson, H. Wheeler. *The Cross in the Old Testament.* Philadelphia: The Westminster Press, 1955.

Robinson, H. Wheeler. *Suffering, Human and Divine.* New York: The Macmillan Company, 1939.

Rowley, H. H. *From Moses to Qumran.* New York: Association Press, 1963.

Rowley, H. H. *Submission in Suffering.* Cardiff: University of Wales Press Board, 1942.

Schaper, Robert N. *Why Me God?* Glendale: G/L Publications, 1974.

Scott, R. B. Y. *The Way of Wisdom in the Old Testament.* New York: The Macmillan Company, 1971.

Scott, R. B. Y. *Proverbs–Ecclesiastes.* Anchor Bible. New York: Doubleday and Co., 1965.

Snaith, N. H. *The Book of Job.* London: The Epworth Press, 1945.

Snaith, Norman H. *The Book of Job: Its Origin and Purpose.* London: SCM Press, Ltd., 1968.

Stevenson, W. B. *The Poem of Job.* London: Oxford University Press, 1947.

Terrien, S. "Introduction and Exegesis of Job." *Interpreter's Bible.* New York: Abingdon Press, 1954.

* Terrien, S. *Job: Poet of Existence.* New York: The Bobbs-Merrill Company, Inc., 1957.

* Tournier, Paul. *Guilt and Grace.* Translated by A. W. Heathcote. New York: Harper and Row, 1962.

Toy, Crawford H. *Proverbs.* International Critical Commentary. New York: Charles Scribner's Sons, 1899.

Twentieth Century Interpretations of The Book of Job. Edited by Paul S. Sanders. Englewood Cliffs: Prentice-Hall, Inc., 1968.

The Voice Out of the Whirlwind: The Book of Job (Materials for Analysis). Edited by Ralph E. Hone. California: Chandler Publishing Company, Inc., 1960.

* Von Rad, Gerhard. *Wisdom in Israel.* Nashville: Abingdon, 1972.

Periodicals

Baab, O. J. "The Book of Job," *Interpretation*, V (1951), 329–43.

Baker, J. "Commentaries on Job," *Theology* LXVI, No. 515 (May 1963), 179–85.

Burrows, M. "The Voice from the Whirlwind," *Journal of Biblical Literature*, XLVII (1928), 117–32.

Goldsmith, R. H. "The Healing Scourge: a study in suffering and meaning," *Interpretation*, XVII (1963), 271–9.

Irwin, W. A. "The Elihu Speeches in the Criticism of the Book of Job," *Journal of Religion*, XVII (1937), 37–47.

Irwin, W. A. "Job's Redeemer," *Journal of Biblical Literature*, LXXXI (1962), 217–29.

Kaufman, Stephen A. "The Job Targum from Qumran," *Journal of the American Oriental Society*, vol. 93, no. 3 (July–Sept. 1973), 317–27.

Knight, H. "Job (considered as a contribution to Hebrew Theology)," *Scottish Journal of Theology*, IX (1956), 63–76.

Kramer, S. N. " 'Man and His God,' A Sumerian variation on the 'Job' motif," *Vetus Testamentum*, Supplement III (1955), 170–82.

Kuyper, L. J. "The Repentance of Job," *Vetus Testamentum*, IX (1959), 91–4.

Laks, H. J. "The Enigma of Job. Maimonides and the moderns," *Journal of Biblical Literature*, LXXXIII (1964) 345–64.

MacKenzie, R. A. F. "The Purpose of the Yahweh Speeches in the Book of Job," *Biblica*, XL (1959), 435–45.

Meek, T. J. "Job xix 25–27," *Vetus Testamentum*, VI (1956), 100–3.

Ross, James F. "Job 33:14–30: The Phenomenology of Lament," *Journal of Biblical Literature*, vol. 94, no. 1 (Mar. 1975), 38–46.

Sarna, N. M. "Epic Substratum in the Prose of Job," *Journal of Biblical Literature*, LXXVI (1957), 13–25.

Taylor, W. S. "Theology and Therapy in Job," *Theology Today*, XII (1956) 451–63.

* Thompson, K. T., Jr. "Out of the Whirlwind. The Sense of Alienation in the Book of Job," *Interpretation*, XIV (1960), 51–63.

Williams, R. J. "Theodicy in the Ancient Near East," *Canadian Journal of Theology*, II (1956), 14–26.

York, Anthony D. "zr'rwm'h as an Indication of the Date of 11 Qtg Job?" *Journal of Biblical Literature*, vol. 93, no. 3 (September 1974), 445–6.

Zink, J. K. "Impatient Job, interpretation of Job 19:25–27," *Journal of Biblical Literature*, LXXXIV (1965) 147–52.

NOTES

Preface

1. Thomas Carlyle, *On Heroes, Hero Worship, and the Heroic in History* (New York, 1905), p. 69.

Chapter 1

1. Marvin Pope, *Job*, Anchor Bible (New York: Doubleday, 1965), p. lxx.

2. On the role of tradition and authority in wisdom, see below p. 26. Also, in special cases, according to the wise men, God reveals his will for individuals through esoteric dreams. One function of the wise men is to interpret dreams. Though Proverbs does not mention dreams, in Daniel and Joseph we find expert practice of this art.

3. For a fuller discussion of these passages and the wisdom-secular viewpoint, see Appendix C, "Wisdom: The New Theology, 1000 B.C."

4. The following presentation is an attempt to systematize Proverbs as an illustration of what is called "orthodox" wisdom. Orthodox wisdom is the more or less consistent point of view found throughout Proverbs and developed further in Sirach. Job and Koheleth stand in opposition to this orthodoxy.

5. Italicized portion translated by the author.

6. The wisdom psalms, especially 37, 49, and 73, express this theme in its greatest development and depth. The most sophisticated and beautiful of these is Psalm 73.

7. Also see Psalms 4; 6; 13; 17; 22; 35:11–18, 19–28; 38; 41; 42; 43; 55; 57; 69; 71; 123. Psalm 55:12–14 speaks of friends

who have become slanderous enemies. Psalms 17 and 26 contain protestations of innocence in the face of such judgment, similar to Job 31.

Chapter 2

1. "Satan" is not used here as a personal name. The Hebrew has the article before the word clearly indicating the term is a title. It should be translated as "the satan" or with the footnote (NEB) "the adversary." He is not the causer of evil but acts as a kind of prosecuting attorney cross-examining God's testimony concerning Job.

2. The most complete analysis I know concerning the language and structure of the prose folk epic is found in N. M. Sarna, "Epic Substratum in the Prose of Job," *Journal of Biblical Literature* 77 (1957): 13–25.

3. It does not, however, read as smoothly as implied in the NEB translation which has rearranged an awkward phrase in 42:10.

4. Those who would view Job as a philosophical dialogue totally miss the motivation for Eliphaz's response. They must interpret Job's speech (chap. 3) as raising a philosophical problem and/or view Eliphaz as overly concerned with divine justice. The positive character of the speech including the allusion to Job's innocence makes it clear Eliphaz seeks to comfort Job by reminding him of his faith.

Chapter 3

1. Italicized portion translated by the author.

2. The only possible exception to this statement is found in 9:22–24. Here Job does directly accuse God of tyrannical injustice. The importance of these three verses should not be overblown. In context Job appears to be trying to prod God into answering. Further he qualifies his statement with the conclusion "if not he, then whom?"—a conclusion that aims the defiance at the friends and would make them blasphemers if they respond. Lastly, it is significant that the friends, who are

extremely sensitive to Job's latent unorthodoxy, never respond to this apparently blatant unorthodoxy.

Chapter 4

1. The interpretation here is that Job rehearses only the theme of what he would say to God (10:2 ff) and then launches into a prayer. If one interprets more of chapter 10 or even the entire chapter as Job's coming speech, this does not substantially change the understandings.

Chapter 5

1. Here and throughout this chapter italicized portions of the biblical text are the author's translations.

2. The biblical text inserts the speeches of Elihu at this point. Reasons for considering them secondary were summarized in chapter three of this book. Clearly the friends' judgment has hardened Job in an attitude of recrimination against God. They must be silent before Job will be open to hear the voice of God, whose judgment is entirely different from the friends'.

3. The Greek Septuagint, which omits the description of the ostrich, the rain in the wilderness, and many of the phrases describing the animals, shows purposeful editing to rewrite God's speech as describing order.

4. The Hebrew *'m's* is not the transitive *m's* ("to despise," RSV and KJV) but is the intransitive parallel of *mss* ("to flow," "to melt," NEB, cf. LXX, Targum, Syriac, and Psalm 58:8). The Hebrew *nḥm* may also be used to mean "to comfort oneself" and "to be comforted." Throughout Job the verb is used in the piel in this sense (2:11, 7:13, 21:34, 29:25, and 42:11). The preposition *'al* is unusual. In Ezekiel 14:22 we find the same phrase *nḥm* *'al* translated "you will be comforted for the harm I have done to Jerusalem." A possible translation of Job 42:6*b*, then, is "I am comforted concerning dust and ashes," i.e., for Job's pain and sorrow.

5. The Behemoth is traditionally understood to be a hippo-

potamus and the Leviathan, a crocodile; however, they also seem to have certain mythological characteristics.

Chapter 6

1. If in 19:26 ff Job does affirm a belief that he will see God after death, then this passage is the culmination of Job's hope for life eternal. However, the desire for vindication is stronger in this passage than the desire for God's love. As we have seen, the desire to preserve his integrity slowly dominated all of Job's thoughts and hopes.

2. The Rt. Rev. William H. Folwell, as told at the Lay School of Religion, St. John's Cathedral, Jacksonville, Florida, January 29, 1974. Used by permission.

Author's Postscript

1. A fuller discussion of the relationship of wisdom and the absence of God is found in Appendix C, "Wisdom: The New Theology, 1000 B.C."

Appendix A

1. On the independence of Ecclesiastes 3:2–8, see G. von Rad, *Wisdom in Israel*, trans. J. D. Martin (Nashville: Abingdon, 1972), pp. 138–9.

Appendix B

1. The total lack of agreement on assigning these chapters to individuals in the dialogue is well illustrated in Norman H. Snaith, *The Book of Job*, Studies in Biblical Theology, 2d ser. 11 (Naperville, Ill.: Allenson, 1968), Appendix, J, pp. 100–3.

Appendix C

1. Gerhard von Rad, *Wisdom in Israel*, trans. J. D. Martin (Nashville: Abingdon, 1972), pp. 58–9.

INDEX OF BIBLICAL REFERENCES